BOW
DOWN

BOW DOWN

LESSONS FROM DOMINATRIXES ON

HOW TO BE A BOSS

IN LIFE, LOVE, AND WORK

LINDSAY GOLDWERT

TILLER PRESS
New York London Toronto Sydney New Delhi

Tiller Press
An Imprint of Simon & Schuster, Inc.
1230 Avenue of the Americas
New York, NY 10020

First Tiller Press paperback edition January 2021

TILLER PRESS and colophon are trademarks of Simon & Schuster, Inc.

For information about special discounts for bulk purchases, please contact Simon & Schuster Special Sales at 1-866-506-1949 or business@simonandschuster.com.

The Simon & Schuster Speakers Bureau can bring authors to your live event. For more information or to book an event, contact the Simon & Schuster Speakers Bureau at 1-866-248-3049 or visit our website at www.simonspeakers.com.

Interior design by Jaime Putorti

Manufactured in the United States of America

10 9 8 7 6 5 4 3 2

The Library of Congress has catalogued the hardcover edition as follows:

Names: Goldwert, Lindsay, author.
Title: Bow down : lessons from dominatrixes on how to get everything you want / Lindsay Goldwert.
Description: New York : Tiller Press, 2020. | Includes bibliographical references and index.
Identifiers: LCCN 2019046242 (print) | LCCN 2019046243 (ebook) | ISBN 9781982130466 (hardcover) | ISBN 9781982130473 (ebook)
Subjects: LCSH: Sexual dominance and submission—Social aspects. | Assertiveness in women. | Control (Psychology) | Self-realization in women.
Classification: LCC HQ79 .G65 2020 (print) | LCC HQ79 (ebook) | DDC 306.77/5—dc23
LC record available at https://lccn.loc.gov/2019046242
LC ebook record available at https://lccn.loc.gov/2019046243

ISBN 978-1-9821-3046-6
ISBN 978-1-9821-3051-0 (pbk)
ISBN 978-1-9821-3047-3 (ebook)

For my nieces,
the world is yours.

I felt luxuriously involved in an unsolvable
mystery, my favorite way to feel.

—EVE BABITZ

CONTENTS

THE POWER OF DESIRE

THE POWER OF THE SPIRIT

AUTHOR'S NOTE

In order to protect their privacy, all the professional dominatrixes are referred to by their professional names unless they've given me their express permission to do otherwise.

BOW DOWN

I'M A MONEY WRITER.
SO WHY WRITE ABOUT KINK?

Question: What do sex, power, and money have in common?

Everyone wants more of it but nobody talks about how to get it.

We think everyone has more of it than we do.

Once we get it, we worry about how to hold on to it.

I've never been your typical money writer and podcaster. When it comes to saving money, I'd rather interview a comedian about her budget woes than talk to a dull financial planner. In 2015, when I debuted *Spent*, a storytelling podcast where interesting people share their biggest money mistakes, I wasn't looking for answers to how Americans could fix their finances. After all, everyone knows how to be better with money: save more, spend less, sacrifice pleasure today for satisfaction tomorrow. There's no one answer as to why we struggle with money. We all have a million little answers for why we can't get it together:

I was sad, so I shopped.

I grew up poor, I was desperate to feel rich.

I didn't want to feel stupid, so I didn't ask questions.

To ask people about their finances is to ask them about

their families, their upbringings, their self-esteem, and their hopes and dreams. This is why so many people spend a fortune to attend "get rich now" workshops and blindly follow money gurus. We all want a set of instructions to teach us how to live our lives. Have you ever dropped hundreds of dollars on home gym equipment or a set of ludicrously intense fitness DVDs that promise to "jump-start" your road to health and hotness? I've done it. I remember being so psyched while typing in my credit card number and then feeling like I'd finally taken control when the package arrived. I would dutifully use whatever I'd ordered for about two days. And then . . . ennui. A week later, the DVDs (or in my case, fitness bands) were moved to my back bedroom, then into a corner, and then to their final resting place in the back of the closet, where they would gather dust.

What did I want from those fitness bands? I thought I was seeking a fun, low-clutter way to work out from home. Here's what I was actually asking them to accomplish: "Help me fix years of self-loathing, feelings of failure, and instilled terror at the hands of gym teachers, mean girls, and internalized ideas of what I think I'm supposed to look like at every age and in every situation. Also, please make me sound smarter at work and give me the strength to cut shitty people out of my life."

That's a lot to ask from a few pieces of orange rubber tubing with flimsy plastic handles.

All of this got me thinking about why I'd always struggled to get what I want in the macro sense. Yes, I wanted to get a handle on my eating habits. Yes, I wanted to have a career that I could be proud of. Yes, I wanted to feel powerful about my finances, have a great sex-filled marriage, and walk and talk with confidence. I began to realize that there was no product or treasure map that would offer me easy solutions to any of the above.

What I was seeking was a philosophy to live by.

■ ■ ■

I've always been fascinated with alternative cultures and people who live one way by night and another by day. In my early twenties, while pursuing my master's in journalism, I performed stand-up comedy in rank basements in order to write a piece about the struggle to get famous. (I'd also go on to perform stand-up comedy in my thirties.) I interviewed a porn star who briefly held the record for having participated in the world's biggest gang bang to learn about what it took to get in (and eventually leave) the adult entertainment industry. When New York City began its crackdown on strip clubs in the early 2000s, I interviewed bikini-clad dancers, no longer allowed to dance topless, about their financial prospects and their next moves. I always believed, and still do, that you can learn more about the human condition from interesting people than from "experts."

This book began as a fun, dishy exercise. Who better to ask about power dynamics at home and in the workplace than a professional dominatrix? It didn't take long for me to realize that this book would be harder to write than I thought. I was in a precarious time in my own life—midcareer, midmarriage, and nearly (ack) midlife. At first I was asking questions that I thought "women" would want to know the answers to. Then I gave up the ghost and started to ask the questions that *I* wished I had the answers to.

When I told men I was interviewing dominatrixes about their work and all the things they've learned about power dynamics, they said, "Whoa, you're gonna learn a lot about whipping dudes."

When I told women I was interviewing dominatrixes about their work and all the things they've learned about power dynamics, they all said, "You're going to have to tell me *everything.*"

I was tired of seeing the word "empowerment" get tossed

around like a tired old Hacky Sack. When everything is "empowering," is anything actually empowering? I was so sick of hearing glib TED Talks, reading treacly personal essays, and seeing the concepts of confidence and strength used as fodder for celebrity-branded yoga mats, cosmetics, and high-priced nutritional supplements. I was also getting increasingly annoyed at a lot of the advice being given to women about how to be more effective in the workplace. So much of it seemed vague and out of touch with the kind of struggles that most of us actually face on the job. Most of it also seemed impossible to take action on, especially if you weren't the one in charge.

I was tired of being told to lean in. I wanted to learn how to say "fuck off."

I didn't want to write a women's empowerment book. I wanted to write about *power*.

■ ■ ■

One of the most interesting things that happened when I was writing this book was how many professional women told me they'd worked as dominatrixes in their past lives. They'd done it to put themselves through grad school, for the thrill of it, or to pay bills during strange times in their lives. I was stunned to learn how many of my peers had spent their days working in the numerous dungeons (many of them gone now) that dotted New York City in the late 1990s and early 2000s.

These women, the ones I met *before* writing this book, had all moved on from their days of throwing floggers, busting balls, spanking, and ordering rich white men to cower at their feet. Now they're executives, professional comedians, editors, and professors. And yet, they all had one thing in common: They were smart, progressive, and cool; funny, empathetic, and nonjudgmental. And they all recalled their days in the dungeon with a fondness. They'd learned so much about themselves, about humanity, and about sexual complexity.

When I started writing this book, I had an idea of what professional dominatrixes did with their clients. I watched videos and interviews, I read memoirs and guides, I looked at fetish sites and dutifully pored over the whips, the canes, the cuffs, and all the other accoutrement. I didn't know anything about the tenets of BDSM or its codes. I knew nothing about how it can shape a lifetime of views on love, sex, relationships, confidence, and inner strength. It wasn't until I met the dommes in person, at events, over coffee, in their homes, and over the phone that I found that I was onto something incredibly valuable. Something beyond sex and power. An ethos for life.

More and more, BDSM and its practitioners are beginning to appear in our popular culture. In addition to working with clients, professional dominatrixes are authors, sex educators, couples counselors, feminists, and activists. Many of the women I interviewed for this book have been quoted in publications like *Cosmopolitan*, *Refinery29*, *Glamour*, *GQ*, *Allure*, the *New York Times*, the *Washington Post*, the *Atlantic*, and many others. The rest of the world is catching on to the fact that pro-dommes know more than just how to perform power—they're also using what they've learned in the dungeon to help others find it for themselves.

■ ■ ■

During my research, I read a lot of books about kink. *A lot.* There are so many good ones out there that explain how to keep your slave submissive, how to be an effective top, and how to talk about consent. I learned about different kinds of rope, why certain floggers are "sting-y" and others are "thuddy." I learned why people love kink, and how it speaks to them as sexual beings.

When I first started getting interested in the world of kink, I was new to all the terminology. Every time a pro-domme or person in "the lifestyle" would use a word or explain a concept, I'd say, "Wow, that's great advice for life!"

I can only imagine how annoying I was. Because I. Was. Very. Excited. To. Ask. Lots. Of. Questions. But I wanted to be careful. Is there anything worse than someone who wants to take your hot sexy thing and make it dull and palatable for the masses? There were so many good lessons that worked both in and out of the bedroom, so much new vocabulary to explain the complexities of power dynamics, vulnerability, communication, self-protection, self-respect, and embracing of selves within ourselves, both erotic and not.

The women I spoke to changed my life. There are so many wonderful pro-dommes and sex workers who are out in the streets fighting to be made visible and protected under the law. The world of kink is progressive, it's inclusive, it's welcoming. I wrote this for beginners (or advanced beginners) who are new to the concept of power dynamics in the context of our everyday lives and want to dig deeper within themselves.

It's for people who may not have been "born kinky" but are definitely "born curious."

WHAT IS A DOMINATRIX?

A dominatrix knows power is not about putting others down or causing pain; true power is the ability to affect positive change in oneself and others.
—SIMONE JUSTICE

The art of domination is a mix of sensuality, performance, empathy, and fantasy interpretation. To explain its complexities, I turned to Simone Justice, one of the most renowned and revered professional sex educators in the world. She travels to dungeons, conferences, and events all over the world to talk about the ethics of kink. Her class, How to Dominate, focuses on the psychological and verbal aspects of skillful domination. She also works to train actors and consults on film and television to ensure accurate portrayal of BDSM.

A teacher first, a dominatrix second, she has spent years honing her personal philosophy of generosity and wisdom-sharing, with a fierce dedication to personal and professional standards.

I asked Justice to explain what it is a professional dominatrix does, how she defines the craft, and to dispel the stereotypes and myths.

For the sake of clarity, unless I indicate otherwise, I've chosen to refer to the women in this book as "professional dominatrixes," or "pro-dommes," to indicate that they do this work for a living as opposed to those who dominate only as part of their personal relationships.

WHAT IS A DOMINATRIX?

Justice defines a professional dominatrix as a female-identified person educated in BDSM technique (bondage, discipline, sadomasochism) who safely, ethically, and skillfully manifests her client's kinky fantasies. The pro-domme does this with such accuracy and care that she earns a premium fee for her rare expertise. This requires a commitment to training, introspection, education, and evolution.

"Advanced precision skills, such as safely and accurately throwing a single tail whip, can take years of classes and practice to develop," said Justice. "There are myriad techniques that the elite dominatrix has dedicated herself to perfecting."

The dominatrix does not live her life by anyone else's rules. She has empowered herself to proudly step outside norms in order to express her own sexuality and, through her work, assist others in doing so. And she uses her own comfort to help clients find and embrace their own sexuality, perhaps to feel, for the first time, desired for who they truly are.

"The dominatrix is an alchemist who transmutes the dark into the light," said Justice. "She knows power is not about putting others down or causing pain; true power is the ability to affect positive change in oneself and others."

A true dominatrix deeply enjoys the feeling of exerting power and control. To be successful and to sustain a career, the desire to dominate must be in her DNA. She knows that being an Alpha woman is different from being a professional dominatrix. One is nature, and the other is work.

"While a dominatrix will feel the rush of complete control in her exalted position, confidently and skillfully wielding her power, she is never selfish or self-aggrandizing because she knows she is merely playing an exaggerated version of herself," said Justice. "Her real power lies within. It's what got her to that temporary pedestal, and it will endure long after playtime is over."

A pro-domme may or may not be kinky in her personal life. She shops for groceries, gets her car fixed, pays her student loans, and laughs and cries with her friends, like the rest of us.

She may identify as straight, lesbian, genderqueer, or nonbinary. Pro-dommes are white, women of color, tall, short, funny, serious. They may also work as models, writers, artists, or film and video directors. They're all entrepreneurs who run their own businesses. While researching this book, I've met pro-dommes who hold advanced degrees in fields including psychology, theater direction, literature, and public health.

The dominatrix is a trope, a myth. A pro-domme is a person who embodies her work. She is a human being. She is a not a collection of stereotypes or a fetish object.

"A dominatrix knows she is not unlike other women," said Justice. "If they only knew they held the same power within themselves."

WHAT DOES A DOMINATRIX DO?

A dominatrix orchestrates a personally tailored BDSM experience. She listens carefully to a client's dreams and fantasies and then uses her knowledge to educate, elaborate, then design a realistic and safe encounter to achieve the longed-for result, and more.

A pro-domme abides by the code of BDSM. These tenets include a strict adherence to the rules of consent, negotiation, safe words, and respect for boundaries and limits. Her professional toolbox, in addition to floggers, clamps, rope, and ball gags, includes kindness, first-rate communication skills, and a world-class imagination. She possesses a wide variety of skills, which can include discipline, impact (hitting with hands or objects), humiliation, body worship, and hundreds of variations on the themes of dominance and submission.

Beyond her technical skills, she must possess insight into the psychological aspects of BDSM and power dynamics and be able to reassure clients that despite their fears their secret passions are not so rare after all.

If there's a fantasy that you believe is so dark and perverse that if you were to voice it, the hand of God would come down and slap you into the bowels of hell, chances are a skilled pro-domme somewhere in the world has heard it already and has accepted it without judgment.

"She will gently open a client's closet of desires and then dissolve the shame," said Justice. "For the client, just the feeling of their hidden self being accepted can be incredibly freeing."

For many clients, it will take more than a single session to uncover their fantasies and realize their true sexual selves. While some clients come once and never return, many professional dominatrixes will see the same clients for months and even years.

"Over time, the safe and nourishing environment that a dominatrix creates leads to pronounced changes. Clients can truly let go and allow their trusted dominatrix to be completely in charge," says Simone.

It is a relationship built on trust.

An expert dominatrix then uses this earned bond during BDSM play to train her client in taking more sensation, or performing better service for her. She introduces them to re-lated BDSM activities that she knows they will enjoy, that will benefit them and expand their horizons. These activities may include cleaning, running errands, keeping a journal of their goals to empower them to achieve a life, sexual and not, that is fulfilling to them. The professional dominatrix can serve as a kind of life coach. She has access to her clients' deepest desires and she can help them get there—if they're willing to submit.

"Dominatrixes use their position to better the lives of their clients and to help them progress toward their goals, all under the umbrella of training the client to be a better servant," said Justice. "She speaks directly, and teaches them not only to fol-low orders but also how to ask for what they want and express themselves clearly."

The relationship between a dominatrix and client is unique. It is a strong bond, and yet, they may never even know each other's real names.

Post-session, the dominatrix will offer aftercare both phys-ical and emotional, tending to the client's needs by offering water, a blanket, and the rare opportunity to talk about their BDSM experience until she is sure the client is ready and safe to return to the outside world in their daily role.

ARE DOMINATRIXES, LIKE, REALLY MEAN AND VIOLENT PEOPLE?

The most common misperceptions are the ones perpetuated by mainstream media and kinky porn that rely on misguided stereotypes for shock value.

"So often, the dominatrix is played as a condescending, power-hungry, leather-clad woman in thigh-high boots eager to stomp on her client's body and ego, causing grievous bodily harm," said Justice. "While there may be some ignorant pro-dommes who follow this ridiculous example, a true pro-domme is almost the complete opposite."

A pro-domme may act "mean" or inflict pain, but in reality, the aspects of BDSM that appear hurtful or cruel are meticulously vetted and artfully applied to serve a counterintuitive result akin to a runner's high and a peaceful bliss. The relationship between the professional dominatrix and her client is far more complex than just dishing out torment. It's an exercise in unguarded pleasure and the joy of deep connection.

The women I spoke to for this book (and I spoke to dozens while researching it) were unbelievably warm, thoughtful, and kind. They do, however, get pissed off about racism, homophobia and transphobia, and people who desire their services but don't want to pay for it. In addition, they proudly identify as and speak out in solidarity with other sex workers. They fight against unjust laws, speak up for those who are powerless, and are fierce supporters of LGBTQ people.

"A dominatrix does not cower in the face of oppression," said Justice. "She is the public face of BDSM and often becomes involved in activism for alternative sexualities."

DO PROFESSIONAL DOMINATRIXES HAVE SEX WITH THEIR CLIENTS?

Clients who seek out the services of a professional dominatrix aren't looking for sex. They are seeking awe.

They desire a sensual experience, but one that involves much more than just genitals and orifices. They want a full body and mind experience, one that allows a vacation from performing, planning, deciding, perhaps even moving or talking. It's not about sex; it's about something deeper, something that goes beyond the everyday act of penetration and orgasm.

"In our patriarchal culture, it is not easy to find a place to revere the feminine with absolute abandon," said Justice. "To throw oneself at the feet of an Amazon, surrender to her whim, openly be overcome with weakness at the sight of a woman's curves in a corset and literally grovel for just a glance from her."

The professional dominatrix offers her male clients an escape from the confining roles of society that may hem them in and alienate them from their desires. Many are tired of having to fit in and conform with the models of "masculinity" and all the trappings that come with adhering to what society tells them about what it means to be a man.

For the first time in his life, a male client may experience freedom from expectation and the chance to uncover a long-lost part of himself.

Said Justice: "As one client said to me, 'I can get sex, I want something much harder to find.'"

SO IS A DOMINATRIX KIND OF LIKE A SEX THERAPIST?

All of the professional dominatrixes agree that the work that's done in the dungeon is no substitute for therapy—even if it may be therapeutic.

A seasoned professional dominatrix can spot a client who may benefit from a session with a professional psychologist instead of, or in addition to, her work. While there may be a "coaching" aspect to her work, a pro-domme is not a trained medical professional. A pro-domme does not take insurance and cannot prescribe medication. But like a doctor, she believes in first doing no emotional or physical harm.

That said, more and more psychologists are studying how BDSM might work in conjunction with therapy to treat trauma, abuse, and PTSD.[1] They are also exploring how experimentation with power dynamics might help couples communicate more effectively.[2]

I'D LIKE TO GET PAID FOR HITTING MEN. SHOULD I BECOME A PROFESSIONAL DOMINATRIX?

First of all, none of the pro-dommes I spoke to for this book do it because they want to "hit men." In fact, many are proud to call their clients their friends. If working out your violent impulses or performing acts of revenge is your aim, professional domination is not for you.

The women who do this for a living are drawn to it; they're nourished by it; they feel very strongly about the work they do. They know it's the human connection and not just the act of inflicting pain that will sustain their careers.

There are societal judgments and dangers that can come with the work. It can be physically and emotionally draining. And while the laws around sex work in the US are slowly changing, they do not receive the protections under the law that other professional women do. Due to stigma and judgment, not all professional dominatrixes are "out" to their friends and family. They are constantly looking over their shoulder to make sure that they're not being followed by potential predators and need to adhere to a strict vetting process. Nearly all of them told me that while the work can be rewarding, it can also be exhausting. While a select few may have decades-long careers and enjoy financial stability, many burn out. It's hard, emotional work and not for the faint of heart.

THESE WOMEN SOUND AWESOME! HOW CAN I MEET THEM?

Elite dominatrixes are kind of like rock stars. They go on tour; they appear on panels and at conventions; they sign books and autographs. They may host workshops, teach at universities, and make appearances at bookstores. You can check out their websites to learn more about what they do and if they may be coming to an event in your area.

WHAT CAN A PROFESSIONAL DOMINATRIX TEACH ME ABOUT POWER?

Read on!

THE POWER OF THE
WORD

THE POWER OF THE

WORD

KINKY WORDS ARE LIFE WORDS

Kink and BDSM are playfulness with the
sexual privileges of adulthood.

—TINA HORN[1]

This is a book about power dynamics and how we can filter our communications and interactions through the tenets of BDSM. But in order to play responsibly during kinky sex (and in life), it all needs to be filtered through the framework of consent, negotiation, boundaries, safe words, and respect.

Later in the book, I'll talk about how BDSM is a great lens to examine our work lives, home lives, as well as our sex lives. But first, before we get there, we need to get down and dirty.

Let's define some terms, shall we?

WHAT IS KINK AND BDSM?

"Kink" is an umbrella term that can encompass almost anything that's seen as outside the norm of "vanilla" sex.

What's vanilla sex? There's no one definition, but one way to think about it is the kind of sex two people have in mainstream, R-rated movies. This can include the standard male/ female positions and, some may argue, oral sex. Some may define vanilla sex as normative sex between two straight people. Others sum it up by saying it doesn't matter who is doing it; if it doesn't involve BDSM, it's vanilla. There's nothing wrong with vanilla sex! Like the ice cream, it can be sweet, delicious, and wonderful. For a lot of us, it can be the perfect way for you and your partner to express sexual desire and intimacy.

Kinky people take a whole different view of sex and sensuality. For example, not everyone believes that the whole point of sex is for both people to have an orgasm. After all, we have wonderful brains that conjure wild and wicked fantasies, and billions of nerve endings (everywhere) that beg to be stroked and teased. Who among us doesn't love ice cream? But some people, kinky people, want some sprinkles on their vanilla ice cream. Or they want rocky road with all the toppings. Or they just want to drip the ice cream down the backs of their partners and watch them squirm while they enjoy the sharp and crunchy cone. I'm losing the metaphor here, but the point is, not everyone likes to have sex in the missionary position.

BDSM isn't just whips and chains (although whips and chains can definitely be part of it). The "B" stands for "bondage." The "D" stands for "discipline." The "S" stands for "sadism." The "M" stands for "masochism." People have been playing with power dynamics for millennia, but it wasn't until the 2000s that "BDSM" became the mainstream, go-to term. Before that it was "B&D" or "S&M."

The definition of "kink" and all those who contributed to its many aspects and contributions to our culture could fill several volumes. For me to attempt to do so in just a few paragraphs would be doing a great disservice to those who have dedicated their life to studying its history. Kink has Eastern and Western roots, from aspects of the *Kama Sutra* to orgies, partner swapping, and voyeurism in the Roman tale *Satyricon*. From the dawn of Christianity, artists have eroticized its rites and rituals, including flogging and submission. The Victorians may have been having sex for procreation at home, but with sex workers, both male and female, they explored other pleasures, such as oral and anal sex, spanking, cross-dressing and other kinds of gender bending, erotic death obsession, and some pretty wild written and visual erotica. Under the complex and draconian Comstock Laws of the late nineteenth and early twentieth centuries, men with a penchant for photos or magazines where women posed in high-heeled, thigh-high boots risked being charged with sending and receiving obscene material in the mail.

"Leather" is another term for a certain kind of kink. The term gained popularity in the 1950s in gay male biker clubs and has continued to be used today, especially in LGBTQ communities, to let others know their kink fetishes and identity.[2]

But when it comes to this book, which is really the intro-to-the-intro to kinky thinking, I believe that it's best to keep it simple.

"Kink and BDSM are playfulness with the sexual privileges of adulthood," said Tina Horn,[3] journalist and host of the sex podcast *Why Are People Into That?!*

People like to say that kink and BDSM are everywhere now, and are totally mainstream. And to some extent that's true. When perusing Rihanna's lingerie site, I discovered I could purchase a riding crop along with a sensible T-shirt bra. Kinky fashion was on display at the 2019 Met Ball. Celebrities wore latex and harnesses and braided their hair to resemble whips. The filmmaker Lena Dunham and the actress Jemima Kirke wore dresses with the words "Rubberist" and "Looner" on them. (A "looner" is a person with a balloon fetish, who gets more and more aroused as the balloon becomes inflated and then, depending on his or her preference, gets off on the *pop*). The Showtime drama *Billions* features BDSM as a core story line, in the marriage of an attorney general and a corporate psychologist. Lifestyle magazines and online sites like *Glamour*, *Refinery29*, and *Cosmopolitan* now write frankly and enthusiastically about fetishes, floggers, dildos, and pegging.

So yes, I'd say that a lot more people are talking about, writing about, and thinking about kinky sex. You can buy a ball gag on Amazon and have it shipped to you in the same box as your cat litter (ew). You can log on to any porn site, type in a few key words, and see things that you never thought you'd see (or may never want to see again).

And yet, many aspects of kink and BDSM are not at all mainstream, to the delight and relief of the people who partake in them. This can include (but are not limited to) extreme role-play, zoophilia, 24/7 master/slave relationship dynamics, the reveling in bodily fluids of all kinds, tickling, wrestling, objectification, consensual gang bangs, consensual dehumanization and sexual torment. At the same time, kink can be sensual. Kink can be thoughtful. It can involve whips and chains, it can involve nothing more than two or more human beings with wild imaginations and descriptive vocabularies. Kinks are like fingerprints, no two are exactly alike—but we all have them. It's a state of mind and an exciting and often breathtaking way to feed our desires.

Kink can allow us to explore the darker sides of ourselves. Maybe you're looking to explore new and exciting sensations, whether it's a feather down your spine, a vibrator held against your clit, or the pull of rope tightening against your partner's wrists. Maybe you want to get into role-play, give up control, or take control from your partner. All these things may be considered kinky but there's so much more than just objects you can purchase or hold in your hand.

But none of this tells you *why* people do it. What do they get out of it? And really, what's the point of receiving a ball gag in the mail if you don't know why you want to use it?

WHY BE KINKY?

I don't know, why breathe air? Why have adventure? Why explore all the wildest recesses of our minds while we're still here on Earth? Why imagine yourself in a position of power that may lead you to believe that you deserve more of it in your daily life? Why explore new sensations and feelings that may turn your idea of desire—and satisfaction—on its head?

Remember these words; you'll be hearing them a lot throughout this book: consent, negotiation, boundaries, safe words, and respect. They form the lens through which we'll be examining the way we interact with the world—how we deserve to be treated, and how we should treat others.

Kink can allow you to explore different parts of yourself and your sexuality without having to lock anything in, without commitment. You can play as you want, explore all your different selves, forage through all your fantasies, while embracing or abandoning fetish or lifestyle "labels."

You can go on a vision quest and come back to who you are afterward. That's pretty cool.

With the right partner or partners, it can be freeing, cathartic, transformative, and hot beyond our wildest dreams. We can show sides of ourselves that we've never dared to show before. We can allow ourselves to be choked, gagged, hit, tied up, humiliated. We can have cocks; we can see what it's like to fuck someone from a completely different perspective. We can choke, gag, hit, tie someone up, humiliate. We can "force" someone to have sex with us; we can explore the fantasy of being "forced."

We can spit on someone; we can be spit on. We can control someone's orgasm; a person can control ours. We can be sex objects; we can objectify others. We can be goddesses, governesses, or mistresses. We can be subs, slaves, or property. We can explore aspects of pain and pleasure; we can inflict them on others.

We can do all this and then return to our regular selves afterward. That's magic.

COULD I BE KINKY?

You may already be, and not even know it.

Maybe one night, while you were having sex doggy style, your partner held your hands behind your back. And you gasped and came extra hard. Or you got on top of your partner, held his arms down, and rode him until you exploded. It's all good, clean, consensual fun, but, newsflash, all that is wading tippy-toe into the banks of Lake Kink. This is because you were getting off on the power dynamic of it all. By letting your partner hold your arms behind your back, you were allowing him to take control. By pinning him down, you were flipping the normative power dynamic and putting your pleasure first.

Many activities and feelings associated with kink may seem scary, but here's the thing—we already harness these concepts in our daily lives. We're already using what's between our ears to bring us to heightened states. If you practice yoga or meditation, you're already accessing these feelings. We follow ritual. We tune into ourselves to bring ourselves to an altered state.

We also know how pain can dissolve into pleasure. A deep tissue massage can hurt, but oh, it can hurt so good. Pushing through a tough workout can have ecstatic rewards. Let's not forget the rush we get from confronting and overcoming fear.

The feeling you get after a terrifying bungee jump or success-fully completing a grueling exam after months of study can only be described as euphoric.

It's not so strange. After all, pleasure and pain are both tied to the interacting dopamine and opioid systems in the brain. The "high" experienced by people who find extreme sensations sexually arousing is similar to what athletes experience when they push their bodies to the limit.

Mistress Couple, author of *The Ultimate Guide to Bondage: Creating Intimacy Through the Art of Restraint*, is a New York–based dominatrix. She's also the former innkeeper at La Domaine Esemar, a luxurious BDSM training château and "bed and dungeon." In between high-intensity sessions with men, women, and couples, she juggled appointment books, planned events, and coordinated workshops with the internationally renowned kink legends who visit La Domaine to teach their special brand of discipline and desire.

"A lot of people wonder why anyone would want to experience pain or enjoy masochism. Most masochists just have a higher pain tolerance than other people," said Mistress Couple. "Martial artists and marathoners are already aware of this, but it's very similar to the feeling that runners get, where you start cramping and you feel like you can't continue, and then you break through that wall and you get that runner's high, that rush, that feeling of satisfaction."[4]

Taking the leap from enjoying intense sensation outside the bedroom to allowing yourself to access it in your sex life—that's kinky. Also kinky? Bringing feelings of sexual power out of the bedroom and into the world.

This doesn't mean showing up to work in full latex and ordering your colleagues to do your work. You can't physically punish a boss for being disrespectful, or demand a raise because you are a Goddess. All of that sounds fantastic, don't get me wrong. But we don't have to be so literal to use kinky tenets to get what we want on the job, at home, and in our relationships.

We'll dive deeper into all of this in later chapters, but asserting dominance, speaking with authority, demanding consent, holding yourself and others to high standards, and highlighting what makes you exceptional versus trying to be like everyone else—these are the keys to becoming a better, smarter, and more powerful you.

Looking at life through a kinky lens means finding satisfaction not by blending in but by embracing all the aspects of what makes you unique and wonderfully weird. When you think kinky, you're embracing a life that's out of the ordinary and creating the rules which you choose to live your life by.

WHAT KIND OF KINKY PERSON AM I?

Back to the bedroom. There's no one way to be kinky.

"Something that I teach a lot in my work is that, whatever your preconception is about BDSM or kink, you have to find your own style. It's the same way you may have a cooking style or a genre of books that you like to read or whatever your craft or your hobby might be," said Tina Horn.

If you've got a sense of humor, for instance, you don't have to lock it away. There's no one way to dominate or submit. There's no one costume, personality, or sensibility. You only have to bring yourself. If you're playful, be playful. If you're meticulous, be meticulous. If you're into fashion, you can let what you wear drive you. Otherwise it can risk feeling alien or wooden—like you're reading from a script rather than acting out a fantasy.

"I myself am an extremely campy dominatrix, and if I'm playing with someone and they want me to be strict and severe and restrained, I can totally do that and even enjoy it, but on the inside, I'm thinking, 'This is hilarious,'" said Horn. "But I can be laughing like that, but then at the drop of a dime, I can be like, 'Get down on your fucking knees.'"

It's kind of like theater. While some actors feel more comfortable playing a certain kind of character, others may be able to slip into others with ease. But the best actors bring themselves to their role. Meryl Streep can play any role in the world, but she's always Meryl Streep.

"Being able to move around so much and be such a chameleon, that shifting quality makes me feel powerful, because it keeps people on their toes," said Horn. "People may not expect that I contain multitudes and that I have these other characters or archetypes within me. Seeing the look on someone's face when they're like, 'Oh shit. I was not expecting to be scared of this person' is a lot of fun."

Maybe you love the shiny toys, the feel of luxury leather, shivery suede, having something customized just for you. If that's your thing, there's no end to the wild accessories you can amass.

"Some people show up to kink events with their bag and they open up it up and they have all these instruments, and that's part of their ritual," said Horn. "They have this kind of braided whip for this kind of thing and this bull hide flogger, but oh, this one is heavier, and so on. They like comparing notes like, 'Oh, I had this custom-made,' or 'My friend has been making these special rainbow glittered whips' or whatever.

"That may be your thing, but it's cool if it's not. I'm very anti-materialist and more of a cerebral and conceptual person in general. I'm just not really a gearhead. But that's not a judgment of people who are."

I, for one, love the fashion and style. I die for the corsets, the accessories, the latex, how it all hugs and shapes the female body. I love the high heels and dramatic makeup, and the cinematic power that it all projects.

"I definitely know people who are into BDSM for the clothes," said Horn. "I used to even act derisive about that, like, 'Oh, that's just superficial. But it's not superficial. It's about the embodiment of the whole thing, it's how they express it. It's about taste, the same way that being a foodie is about taste."

You can be game. You can be giving. But you have to feel good about what you're doing. Otherwise, you're not being kinky; you're just doing what another person wants you to do.

Say your partner wants you to say horrible things to him, demean his genitals, and hit him with a hairbrush. And you're game! You want to try new things; you want to make him happy. But if it ultimately doesn't do anything for you, it's going to feel forced. You'll run out of things to say. You'll dread it. But maybe you can talk about it and come up with a compromise that you can both feel good about.

Hence, the most important rule when finding your kink style: Know thyself.

"If you don't even know yourself, and who you are and what you like, how can you possibly play with somebody on that level?" said Mistress Ava Zhang, a New York City–based pro-domme and writer. "I mean, if you can't even control your emotions and your actions, how can you possibly try to control someone else?"

WHAT IS CONSENT?

"Consent" is an essential term in kink. It means that you and your partner are all in for whatever is going to happen in a scene (the accepted BDSM term for a play session). Anything that's been agreed on beforehand is fair game. This can be anything from spanking to degrading words, dark fantasy exploration, bondage, or anything else two or more wonderfully pervy partners can cook up between them.

Let's say you and your partner want to get into some filthy fun. You're both down to explore sensory deprivation (a blindfold, for example), but one of you isn't into choking or pain. The blindfold is a go but the choking or pain, at least for the partner who says it's a hard no, is strictly off-limits. It would be a hideous violation of consent to go out of these agreed-on boundaries.

This is how people have a *lot* of fun in bed, because there's trust. If the rules of consent are respected, then everyone gets what they want. That trust must be earned, but in an ideal situation, there's no end to the sensual and erotic possibilities that two (or more) people can experience.

■ ■ ■

People who practice BDSM must abide by the rules of consent, but you don't have to be kinky to demand it from others. Consent is black and white. If we've been drinking too much, we cannot consent to sex. Or if someone slips something in our drink, we cannot consent to sex. Or if we've consented to sex in the past but on one particular night can't, or don't, no one is entitled to our bodies.

Yet politicians and mass media coverage insist that consent is a blurry and confusing issue. In 2019, former vice president Joe Biden grossed out a lot of women by blowing off complaints about his overzealous hugging. Instead of attempting to understand where women were coming from, he made a "joke"[5] onstage about asking "permission" to hug Lonnie Stephenson, the male president of the International Brotherhood of Electrical Workers union.[6] Of course, the audience of mostly men laughed. Ha ha ha.

Here's how I once explained consent to a guy who just didn't get it. "Imagine we are both in bed, naked. Suddenly, you come down with horrible diarrhea or the flu. But I kept climbing on top of you and pressing down on your stomach, insisting that you fuck me, even though you're sweaty and sick. And I kept breathing beer breath in your face, trying to push your limp dick inside me while you're desperate to get to the bathroom." The guy grabbed his stomach and said, "Ugh, that sounds horrible. What kind of a monster would do that?"

If only someone slipped a pamphlet explaining "diarrhea" consent to every frat boy, university president, government official, and judge in the world. But consent is not a slippery slope in sex, love, or business. And it fucking sucks that we have to constantly lay down the law.

Our consent and space are violated every day. Back to hugging. If you're a nice person, you may just sigh and deal with it. I am a hugger. And yet, I do not like to hug people I do not feel like hugging. When I started doing stand-up comedy and was thrilled to be making new like-minded weirdo friends, a male comic, mid-hug, took it upon himself to slide his hands under my shirt and knead my muffin-top.

Kindergartners know what a hug is; it's not a new and stunning concept. My hugs say, "I'm happy to see you." To assholes, it means, "I'm happy to touch you."

After-work drinks can be a minefield. How many times have you stood uncomfortably when a drunk coworker or boss "went in for a hug" when you didn't feel like having his parts pressed against you? We brush these occurrences off as simply "awkward" or "gross," but really, they're a violation of your consent. Is your boss a sex criminal? Jesus, let's hope not. But you should be in control of who gets to touch you.

Don't feel like bobbing and weaving to avoid a hug? Handshakes may seem awkward, but a high five followed by a quick exit has worked for me. It also works with a boss who may be clueless about boundaries. "How's it going, _____?" "How's it going, friend?" gets the message across to a coworker that you're happy to greet them with your words versus their hands. Happy hour can be a very unhappy hour if you ever felt obligated to humor an inebriated jerk who got handsy after tossing back a few.

Demanding consent means never having to say, "I didn't want to make it awkward."

If a relationship with a coworker or boss becomes awkward because you've chosen not to accept a close-body embrace, that's a major red flag and something you should start making notes on so you can begin to make a case for yourself with your human resources department.

It may feel unnatural at first. We may not "want to cause a scene" or "make a big thing out of it," but by getting used to the concept of consent, by incorporating it into our way of life, we can shove back the full force of our beings. You can push back against a dude who presses up against you on public transit. When consent is part of what you demand from daily encounters, you can throw the hammer when a date starts to whine about using a condom because you do not and will not consent to unprotected sex.

And consent prompts you to examine the ways you interact with people too. Maybe you aren't as considerate of other people's boundaries as you think you are. I once had a female friend who loved to get drunk and grab my boobs at parties. I laughed it off, but it was actually pretty embarrassing. When she'd shout, "Nice tits!" other people would turn to look. Then it really wasn't so funny.

Consenting to sex once doesn't give someone an all-access pass from now into perpetuity. Just because you consent one night doesn't mean you ever have to do it the next. It's your prerogative to change your mind. There are cases in life when we have no control over who gets to touch us, and those can be horrible and traumatizing. But there are moments in our everyday lives that we can and must use our voices to take control of who gets to touch us and when.

WHAT IS NEGOTIATION?

Say you and your partner consent to have sex with each other. Nice! So, what do you want to do?

So many of us just hop into the sheets and let it unfold the way one person wants it to go—which is fine, until you wonder why one of you thinks the night went well and the other one is left wanting. You may not want to do a certain position, or be put on the spot about whether you want to have anal or oral sex. Maybe you're just looking to be kissed and held, or maybe you want to throw down and have the most wild, uninhibited night of your life. No wonder two people can be in the same bed with completely different ideas of what hot sex is.

This is where negotiation comes in.

Rather than rolling the dice, you can just start off by asking, "What are you into?" Or you can take the wheel and start by saying, "Okay, here's what I'm into." A good and attentive partner will be excited and relieved. After all, no one is a mind reader. And it's hot! Telling your partner what turns you on makes it clear that you know what you like and you're comfortable asking for it. Even better: "Here's what I'm into in general; here's what I'm down to do tonight."

Then, it's up to you to listen to what your partner has to say. We can all have great sex with ourselves, but great sex with others requires listening, empathy, and communication. Once you say what you want, make sure you're clear on what your partner wants.

Negotiation is a key tenet of BDSM. It's what allows people to safely dive into new roles, sensations, and scenarios. "Negotiation ensures that all bases are covered—that everything that could come into play in the scene is discussed beforehand and the boundaries of consent are very clear," writes Mistress Couple in *The Ultimate Guide to Bondage: Creating Intimacy Through the Art of Restraint.*[7] "Moreover, a thorough negotiation gives participants in a scene more of an opportunity to understand and empathize with each other beforehand, which can be very helpful in facilitating in-scene connection."

Empathy is essential to great sex, whether kinky or vanilla. How can you explore each other's desires without really understanding where they're coming from? These are the things that bring us closer together. Negotiation lets you put it all out on the table so that nothing (literally or metaphorically) comes out of nowhere to ruin anyone's good time or, worse, cause harm.

Negotiation is the time to lay out your rules regarding safe sex. To use or not use a condom shouldn't be an anxious battle of will he or won't he in the heat of the moment. This should absolutely be established before the encounter so that everyone is clear.

Negotiation isn't about confrontation. It's about communication, expectations, courtesy, and respect.

This isn't just a tool to ensure better communication in bed. It can also help you in the workplace.

You have the right to know what is expected of you, just as your boss has the right to give you more or less responsibility. A good managerial relationship allows for conflicts, and resolves them in a way that keeps everyone productive and doing their best work. If you're unclear about what you're supposed to be doing during the day or you're unsure about what task to perform first, a good manager should be available for a gut check so you can both prioritize and make sure your time is being used productively. This way, you both know at the outset what needs to get done without any question or confusion.

Negotiation can also translate into a way to keep the peace at home.

Think about the division of labor in your household. Who does the chores? Who buys the groceries? Are you satisfied with your partner's contribution? Outline it all (on paper) and try to come up with a balance that works for both of you. If something comes up, and it needs to be changed, that's fine. But one person can't just let their obligations slide and leave the other person holding the bag. By adopting the BDSM model of negotiation in the rest of our lives, we can ensure that everyone gets to speak their minds and explain what's working (and not working) for them, and how things can go smoothly if one person does X and the other one does Y. The best part: Things can always be renegotiated later on.

Kink is also about accountability. Everyone has to stick to what's been agreed on, or else there's no trust. And if there's no trust, it won't work.

WHAT ARE SAFE WORDS?

"Imagine that you have a fantasy of being submissive, of surrendering, of being captive, of being someone's pet, of being someone's plaything, being someone's toy," said Horn. "Or you have a fantasy of taking control of someone who wants to feel that physical, kinetic energy of force or a psychological fantasy of force. That can be really hot."

But if any of the above were to happen without consent, negotiation, and respect for limits, boundaries, and safe words, it goes from dark or transgressive exploration to sexual assault, physical and emotional abuse, rape, and/or battery. Hitting someone, fucking someone, restraining someone, or humiliating someone without their consent or after they've stopped consenting is a crime.

Safe words are how kinky people stop a scene when things become too much. It's a way to bring things back to earth for a hard reset. They are also what prevent kinky sex (or any kind of sex) from becoming emotional or physical abuse or assault.

We all have dark sides to our subconscious, and wading into them requires a lot of trust and self-knowledge. That's why BDSM requires safe words, so that no one's consent is violated. If you invoke your safe word, everything stops. Partners check in with each other immediately and address the issue. It's a way to dive into our depths with a lifeline.

The best safe words are simple and easy to say. In the kink community, it's popular to abide by the traffic light system. Yellow means "I'm reaching my limit. This is okay but I can't take much more." Red means "stop the scene, right now." To not respect "red" is to cross the line from intense consensual sexual experience to assault.

Whatever word you choose, it has to be clear to all parties and easy to remember and say in the heat of an intense moment. A safe word can be one word; a simple, clear, and effective way to say, "I need this to stop, I don't like what's happening." Sometimes, if you're in the middle of a hot scene and your partner is consensually "forcing you," the word "stop" may not be an effective safe word. Because maybe you don't actually want the other person to stop; it's part of the fantasy. Sensation play can be emotional; it can bring tears. But if those tears are cathartic, the tears aren't a good "safe word."

Safe words shouldn't just be reserved for kinky sex. Consensual vanilla sex can also go from "oh baby" to "I really hate this." How many of us have silently wished sex would just end already, gritted our teeth, or just disassociated, rather than speaking up about physical or emotional discomfort? It's hard to find the words in the moment to express why we're suddenly feeling uncomfortable or unhappy or freaked out in the middle of sex. It's so often a mix of feelings—enjoying the intimacy but not enjoying a certain position, feeling pressure to have an orgasm because your partner is down there on a mission, or feeling resentful when you're not really in the mood.

A safe word can put the situation on pause so you and your partner can check in, stat. Once you're back on the same page, you can either get back to it or call it a night. Either way, you never have to grin and bear it (ever) and your partner is crystal clear on what not to do next time.

Here are examples of safe words that are *not* effective, if you are engaging in any kind of consensual sex or sensual play with a lover:

- "I'm feeling weird."
- "I don't know about this."
- "I'm okay, I think."
- "Could you not?"
- "It's fine."

These words may be conveying how you feel, but they're not effectively communicating your desire to stop what's happening because you're not comfortable.

If you don't want to use a safe word, it's essential to use action words (and say them loud) to tell your partner that you need things to end. No matter what word or words you choose, they should be negotiated beforehand so everyone knows exactly what they mean.

Safe words can keep everyone on the same page during sex,

but more importantly, they protect your safety, feelings, and physical well-being.

Safe words are something to think about outside the bedroom too. You can use them to inform your partner, friends, and others that you have limits, and that you want to be able to communicate them quickly and clearly.

Say you're out with friends and you suddenly feel too drunk to make a responsible decision about getting behind the wheel, going home with a stranger, or continuing to drink. Just say the words and your friends will know that you are in distress and need help, now.

The gym is a place where we can feel pushed past our limit. Fitness experts and personal trainers like to shout at us to "push past the pain," but I know the difference between feeling the burn and feeling like I'm going to faint or puke. A safe word puts you back in control of your body and your emotions. As someone who has both thrown up and fainted at the gym, I wish now I'd had the courage to speak up instead of blaming myself for being "out of shape" or "weak."

Safe words are also a great way to communicate to the people we're with that something that sounded fun at the time has suddenly become a very bad idea. This can include a hike that has ventured too far into the woods, a threesome, or a social situation where you feel endangered due to your gender, religion, sexual orientation, or race.

This is a great lesson to teach our kids, nieces, or nephews. If their peers are about to do something dangerous, like steal, buy drugs, or engage in violence, they can utter their safe word to their closest friend and know that they have an ally. If they don't have a friend close enough to share their safe word with, it may be a sign that they're not hanging out with the right people.

Safe words give us permission to comprehend that we're

at our limit and that we need to stop trying to solve things on our own. It can be a way to "break the emergency glass" in our minds and tell ourselves that it's okay to stop and ask for what we need.

YOUR WORDS, YOUR POWER

Here's what BDSM is not: nonconsensual sex.

This is so important.

There is nothing more devastating than allowing yourself to be vulnerable with someone who violates your trust. It doesn't matter whether you're in a kinky relationship or a vanilla relationship, your consent can be violated.

This is a life lesson. Throughout this book, we'll be talking about how we can speak up for ourselves and make consent and boundaries part of our everyday lives. Yes, we'll be talking about sex, but more importantly, it's about flipping the whole power dynamic in our favor.

No one deserves to feel powerless.

No one deserves to have their consent violated.

No one deserves to be hurt or victimized.

You deserve the right to live and love and express your sexuality as you choose.

Maybe one day, all the assholes of the world will bow down to us. But until then, we must keep working to ask for what we want and need, and never accept less from others than we would ask of ourselves.

LESSON #2

YOU MUST SPEAK
WITH AUTHORITY

"Bitch" is another word for "boss."

—DIA DOMINA DYNASTY

Why is it so hard to say "I want"? Why is it so hard to say "I need"?

Here's a bit about me. I'm a professional writer and journalist who has worked in New York City for more than fifteen years. I've worked for big publications and news outlets, including *Redbook*, *Glamour*, ABCNews.com, and the *New York Daily News*. Recently, I've been working as a money writer and editorial director for start-ups, where I help beginners learn how to invest and save money. I also performed stand-up comedy in NYC for over five years, until I realized that, as much as I loved it, I was a better writer than a performer. I'm married to a very nice man, no kids, one cat.

Over the course of my career, I've worked the overnight shift during presidential elections, covered celebrity deaths, started my own podcast, and authored dozens of articles about everything from hangover cures to navigating workplace bathroom shame. I've made a lot of big life decisions over the course of the last three decades, and yet, I still felt like I was constantly on my back foot. I dealt with change as it came at me, I didn't do a good job getting out in front of what I wanted and needed. I struggled with being an advocate for my ideas. I was great at saying "would it be okay if" but I had a lot of trouble saying "I want" because I wasn't sure what I deserved.

Since beginning work on this book, I've been keeping track of all the times when I've wanted or needed something specific but used wishy-washy language—and then walked away feeling like I'd asked a favor instead.

I wanted to say, "Ugh, this expensive plate of pasta is cold and smells like Alpo." Instead I said, "Everything is great."

I wanted to say, "Those dates don't work for me." Instead I said, "I can make it work."

I wanted to say, "I can't do this task, it's too much." Instead I said, "I'll see what I can do."

I wanted to say, "You hurt my feelings." Instead I said, "I'll be okay."

I wanted to say, "Fuck you." Instead I said, "No worries."

It was just way easier to say something pleasant than to worry about coming off as mean or—gasp—bitchy. It was easier to take care of other people's feelings than to express my own, for fear of confrontation or getting a shitty response. It was easier to seethe than worry that I was acting like a drama queen. It was easier to eat a pint of ice cream than to give someone the finger.

I said "I don't know" when I *did* know. I acted indecisive out of courtesy. I deferred to other people when I knew that they were wrong or that I'd regret it. I've taken calls with recruiters for jobs that I didn't even want and feigned enthusiasm out of politeness. I once tweeted a joke that said "My epitaph will read, 'Ha, no problem'!" A lot of women liked and RT'ed it because they *got* it. Because "ha-ha, no problem" is easier than saying "Thanks for wasting my time."

It's ludicrous how much time we as women waste in an attempt to not come off like we're demanding too much.

I could fill another whole book with examples of women who have been slapped back for sounding too confident. In a study of women in tech,[1] surveyors found that they frequently received criticism about being "judgmental," needing to "adjust their tone," and sounding "abrasive." Men are often told to be *more* aggressive, while women are advised to step back and listen more.[2] Nowhere is this more obvious than on the political stage. Remember when Hillary Clinton got dragged for being "overprepared" for her debate with Donald Trump? A 2010 study indicated that while both male and female politicians were described as "power-seeking," only in women was this perceived as a negative thing.[3]

"The 2010 study didn't just find that female politicians were seen as less caring. It found this perception inspired moral outrage in both male and female study participants, who viewed such women with contempt, anger and/or disgust," writes Caroline Criado Perez in her book[4] *Invisible Women: Data Bias in a World Designed for Men.*

In general, women have a lot more pressure to be "prosocial," meaning they need to constantly walk a tightrope of appearing warm and caring, while also working their way up and holding on to whatever power they amass.

In 2019, we love to applaud women who "give no fucks," who say what they mean and speak truth about racism, sexism, oppression, and gender inequality. And yet, our genuflecting cries of "Yass queen," "She said that," and "Damn, girl" may illustrate our own desire to have the courage to speak so boldly about ourselves and our accomplishments. Instead of leaning on other, more powerful women to say the things we only wish we could say, we can start changing the way we ask for things.

So how could I begin to ask for what I wanted? After all, the very nature of a professional dominatrix's job is to give clear instructions and direct orders.

"Are you asking permission to live your life, or are you just letting people know how you're living? Those are the things I ask myself," Mistress Ava Zhang said. "I don't ask permission. I state what I want."

For Zhang, it begins with daily interactions that can eventually bleed into speaking powerfully everywhere else.

"Let's just say you and I met at a restaurant, and a waiter comes and asks what you want, and you want coffee. How would you ask for that? That tells me a lot about your level of confidence, and your position and control that you have in your life," she said. "Before I became a pro-domme, I would ask, 'Do you think I could have a cup of coffee?' 'When you get a chance, could I have a coffee, please?' 'May I please have a cup of coffee?' I was asking permission. But I don't need to ask a server permission for coffee. It's their job to bring me coffee."

We can start with the small things, and then build up our courage. It can start with a cup of coffee.

START TO SAY "I WANT"

In the world of BDSM, a lot can go wrong if you don't clearly assert what you want. If you're in a submissive role, failing to state your limits can result in serious emotional or physical harm. The same is true for a person in a dominant role who doesn't want to be pressured into performing a scene or action. Both parties need to speak clearly and confidently about their boundaries and not give in to what the other wants. Clear language is an essential element of kink.

Kinky people, like the rest of us, may want to please their

partner by being "open" to what he or she wants to do in bed. That's great, but without clear communication, things can veer off the tracks.

Say a woman is happily taking on the role of submissive, and gets off on verbal humiliation. That's great, but what does that mean? Stacy may like to be called a "dirty little slut" but definitely doesn't want to be called "fat" or "stupid." On the other hand, Jane may cringe at the word "slut" but gets pleasure out of being degraded for her appearance. Some words can elicit good shivers and other ones can trigger painful memories or hurt feelings. A trans person may have triggers associated with being touched or having attention called to certain places on the body. Even if you're in a submissive role, you still have to be your own advocate.

When researching this book, I attended a public workshop and got to hold an actual flogger in my hand. At an event in Brooklyn, I stood behind a willing male who waited anxiously for me to throw the leather tassels hard against his bare flesh. I was in the dominant role because I held the tool of impact. But the whole thing was actually making me feel really anxious. I didn't feel like I had the skills to hit someone safely and "effectively." BDSM is incredibly intimate and I wasn't comfortable at all performing it with a stranger. I was standing in front of a lot of people, so I felt pressure from him and the crowd to give them what they wanted. I wasn't feeling dominant at all. I felt like a fish out of water and I wanted to stop. So I got up the courage to say, "I'm not enjoying this," and I handed the flogger to another woman, who happily reared back and let it crack against the guy's ass while he yelped with ecstasy. It reminded me that no matter what role you want to take on in bed or in life, it can be hard to say no to a pushy person.

If I'd kept going, it would have subverted the whole power dynamic and defeated the point of the experience. If I couldn't speak like a boss with an implement of pain in my hand, what hope did I have of asking for more money for a writing assignment or negotiating a raise?

Lucy Sweetkill and Dia Domina Dynasty (we'll meet her later) are New York City–based pro-dommes and the founders of the kinky play space La Maison du Rouge. The two became close friends after working together for four years at a dungeon. Their friendship led to a shared philosophy and a desire to create a unique space deeply rooted in their ethos of communication, education, wellness, spirituality, and kink. Their goal is to elevate BDSM and foster community through intersectional discourse and the sharing of personal narratives.

Their work is inspired by a need to normalize alternative sexualities, challenge social norms, and bolster a culture around consent and open communication.

Sweetkill and I discussed the power of speaking with confidence over coffee at Hu Kitchen, a healthy eatery near NYU's Greenwich Village campus.

"Saying 'I want' is very hard for women. We're not raised to say these words with confidence," said Sweetkill. "Instead, we say, 'It would be great if you could . . .' 'Would you mind if . . .' We have to train ourselves to say we *want* things."

The longer we spoke, the more I began to think about all the times I asked for permission for ridiculous things. Once, at an airport, I asked the woman next to me if I could use the empty outlet at a charging station. Why? She didn't own the outlet; she wasn't using it. Of course she said yes, but why did I give a complete stranger the power to reject my using a public outlet?

At the doctor, I've asked, "Is it okay if we discuss my concerns about my IUD?" Why wouldn't it be okay? And what if he said no? Sure, maybe he only had time to speak to me about my cold and he could have asked me to make another appointment. (Note: He didn't.) But why did I give someone the option to inconvenience me? I should have said, "I have a question about my IUD." Because it's his job to answer these kind of questions.

How insane is it that I was asking permission to ask questions in the first place? There was no need to self-consciously tippy-toe.

Yes, there are times to ask permission to do something that you can easily do. For example, it's never a good idea to just pet someone's dog or cat. While some pet owners are snooty about who gets to touch Miss Fluffers, sometimes it's about your safety. It gives the owner a chance to say "Go for it" or "Ack, better not, she doesn't like strangers." Same with hugging or picking up someone's kid. Someone's child may have a cold, or the parent may not feel like worrying about whether you're going to drop him. Sometimes asking for permission is courteous and, more importantly, respectful of boundaries. There's a difference between asking for what we want and being rude or inconsiderate. But for the most part, in our daily interactions, we're wasting valuable time and diminishing our power when we ask for permission for things that don't require it.

Rephrasing questions in the form of statements is an easy way to start to speak more powerfully. Before you speak, pause for a moment and ask yourself if you really need permission or if you're just in the habit of soliciting it. Your boss will be happy to accept your report if you say "Here's my report" instead of "Can I give you this report you asked for?" Plus, it saves everyone an email, which is a win for all parties.

All of this takes practice. Even professional dominatrixes, when they're starting out, have to learn to speak assertively. Lucy Sweetkill mentors women who are training to become pro-dommes and teaches them how to speak more clearly and directly to clients. Her tips were just as valuable to someone working in an office or looking to make themselves heard in a crowd.

"When I'm mentoring dommes, I tell them to write things down that you would say that make you feel like you're being dominant," she said. "Just write them down, because when you think them, say them, write them down, they become more a part of you, and easier to say.

"I have them practice saying 'I want.' 'I want you to do this.' 'I want you to bend down. I want you to turn around. I want you to close the door after you come out of the restroom. I want you to put on your shirt. I want you to have a drink of water.'"

When you do this, you'll start to feel the power dynamic of everyday situations change. It may feel scary at first. While attending another workshop, I (nicely, but firmly) ordered a man to kneel in front of me. When he did it, I felt like an imposter. I actually felt panic. Who was I to give an order to another adult? It felt really strange, like I'd ventured into another dimension. Was this real life?

But then I started to get used to it. Now I just use the damn empty outlet because it's mine for the taking.

YOU WILL LEARN TO MANAGE DOWN

Again, it's all about action phrases. A pro-domme must give clear and thorough directions to her client so he knows exactly what she expects him to do. He wants to give up control and he wants to please her. He wants to know how to sit, stand, and kneel. Any confusion will throw off the rhythm of the scene and cause frustration for the pro-domme and her client.

At the same time, most clients aren't dummies. Many are white-collar professionals who are used to being in control during their daily lives. They are paying top dollar to be told what to do without worrying that they're misinterpreting what's being asked of them.

They're not being given requests. They're orders given with confidence and authority.

"With my clients, I don't assume that they know, but I also don't assume that they don't know. I'm not talking down to them, I'm just being very clear about what I want them to do," Sweetkill said. "I'll say, 'Come on in. I want you to put your bag down. Go ahead and use the restroom if you need to, but make sure to close the door right when you're done. When you're settled, I left some water out for you. Have some water, and then come meet me inside.'"

She's very specific to avoid confusion and to set the tone for the session. If she just said, "Come on in, get settled," the client would have to ask if he could put his bag down, if he could use the restroom, and if it was okay for him to go inside the room where the session will happen. This is confusing. Clear language ensures the client knows what's expected of him and she can feel more confident that everything will begin on time. Most important, she has asserted her dominance before the session has even begun.

"It's important to be calm and direct, she said. "I avoid using fillers like 'So I was thinking . . .' and 'I think it would be great if . . .' and 'I was hoping that . . .'"

There's an art to being direct while also being courteous. I once had a very competent HR person who went out of his way to make job applicants feel at home, while also making sure that no one's valuable time was being wasted. Right away, he'd tell you where your meeting would be, where to sit, where the restroom was, and how long you could expect to wait.

It made sense. A job applicant is already confused and nervous. Imagine not knowing where to sit and whether or not you should wait to be seen or if you should get up and knock on a door. No one wants to ask where the bathroom is; it feels like kindergarten. With a direct approach, the company appears to be run by competent people, and the candidate will be in a more confident headspace when the interview begins. Giving too many specifics may feel like you're being condescending, but it can actually made others feel secure and taken care of. There are clear situations where it's okay to tell people what to do.

When you want to speak with authority, don't think of it as talking down to people, but that you're giving very clear direction so that you both get what you need.

Action words can sound alien coming out of our mouths if we've never used them before. Sweetkill recommends using a tape recorder to hear how you sound when you're asking for things.

"I did a lot of debate when I was younger, and to get confident speaking in front of a crowd I recorded myself to see and hear all the little things I was doing that could undermine my words," she said. "It's the hardest truth. All the things you don't notice, the 'ums' or your body language, you have to confront it."

There's nothing more horrifying than listening to the sound of one's own voice. When I started doing stand-up comedy, I'd record my sets and then go into cringe convulsions after hearing all my "ums," "ohs," and "so anyways." When I listened (sometimes in the fetal position), I heard how often I stepped on my own jokes and didn't pause to let people laugh, which caused them to miss the opening of my next joke, which would then get no laughs. My tone was so halting and questioning I seemed like I was begging the audience to laugh rather than assuring them that they were about to have a good time. Comedy audiences home in on weakness right away. They came to be entertained, and having to sit through someone without confidence can be a downer. If you come off as stumbling or apologetic, they'll start talking among themselves and barely notice when you've left the stage.

Sweetkill's advice: Suck it up and face yourself, literally and figuratively.

Interview coaches will offer the same kind of advice. By practicing and foreseeing questions that may come up, you can effectively answer them when you don't have the information in front of you. It can help keep you on track and from sounding flustered. You can hear how your voice trails off or gets high and squeaky. Best of all, you can practice speaking emphatically when touting your achievements, while leaving space for the interviewer to speak and ask questions.

DEMAND ACCOUNTABILITY

It's one thing to ask for something with confidence. It's another to ensure that you'll get what you ask for. How effective can your requests be if no one listens?

Hudsy Hawn is a Los Angeles–based pro-domme, as well as an author and sex coach. As her name suggests, she looks a lot like the actress Kate Hudson, except with flame-red hair and the hourglass figure of a 1950s movie star. Her employment resume has ranged from "Disneyland to the Dungeon" (she performed in rock 'n' roll cover bands for theme park attendees). In addition to teaching workshops for aspiring pro-dommes, she also works with couples and mainstream audiences, helping them find their kink Zen. She's appeared on television and radio and has written for dozens of publications, including *Men's Health*, *Cosmopolitan*, and *Trans Mag*. In 2018, Hawn, also known as "the singing dominatrix," starred in *From Vanilla to Kink*, a one-woman show and a musical memoir.

In early 2019, Hawn and I met up in Los Angeles at Dom-Con, a twice-yearly convention for dominatrixes to meet, bond, share skills, take workshops, and party. In addition to DomCon, conveniently located near the airport, the hotel was also hosting a meeting of the Christian Fellowship Church, a group of Oreck vacuum dealers, and the annual gathering of a company that sold something called customer engagement business processing outsourcing software. The hotel restaurant was filled with vacationing families, men and women in business attire typing on their laptops, and of course, latex-clad dominatrixes holding court during happy hour. I had just come from an astonishing workshop on the art of sensual tease and denial (the seductive art of giving the client just enough to make him crazy but never enough of what he's really craving). Hawn cheerfully flagged me down and we found a cozy table near a window, where we could watch hotel guests gawk at the statuesque women who strode through the lobby in thigh-high boots and the men who walked behind them, dutifully carrying their bursting luggage.

Over drinks, we talked about the art of demanding accountability in a way that gets results. Just as Lucy Sweetkill told me, Hawn said that she built up her communication skills through years of work and practice as an elite dominatrix and teacher.

"You can't just watch a bunch of YouTube videos and then all of a sudden become a dominatrix," Hawn said.[5]

When it comes to giving orders, she recommends speaking slowly and not overloading your audience with too much information. Just a few well-ordered tasks at a time can yield better results. Whether you're leading a meeting or leading a client around on a leash, sometimes less is more. Hurling too many ideas at a person can cause confusion or dilute the one key lesson you're trying to impart.

"There are usually three basic things, actions, or concepts you can give someone to start off with," she said. "You can build from there, but you wouldn't just throw twenty things at them at once," she said.

It's always best to focus on a few key points rather than overwhelm your audience with—to quote Joseph II, the Holy Roman emperor in the film *Amadeus*—"too many notes."

So what does a good BDSM session have in common with an effective business meeting? It's concise, everyone knows what they're supposed to say and do, and it ends on time with all the key issues resolved. This is highly relatable for anyone who's suffered through a "quick" meeting that devolves into chaos due to disorganization and pointless tangents.

Just as bosses have to hold their employees accountable for their work, employees have to "manage up" to make sure they're getting everything they need to get the job done. This is also true for kinksters, whether they're seeking the services of a professional dominatrix or living the lifestyle 24/7.

Whether it's pegging or a performance review, it's always best to put things on paper.

"Don't just shake on it," said Hawn. "By keeping an actual record of what's been discussed, no one can say, 'I didn't agree to that' or 'I don't remember saying this.'"

This keeps everyone honest until you decide it's time to renegotiate.

"Before every session, I write exactly what has been discussed and agreed upon on a whiteboard. I ask him, 'Is this still good? I'm not going to do anything else, no matter how much you beg me,'" she said. "And that's what we do. We stick to that."

Accountability goes both ways. Another reason to write it

all down is so you have evidence to refer to when *you* did what you're supposed to do.

"I'm a submissive at heart," said Hawn. "In my personal relationships, I've met (male) doms who didn't follow up with me or remember important things I said. It made me lose respect for them."

Keeping receipts keeps everyone honest. No one wants to feel gaslit.

A good boss keeps tracks of the tasks she's assigned each of her direct reports. If an employee doesn't follow through with the tasks, he may find himself out of a job. To wit, a dominatrix may also assign tasks to her sub or slave. It can be anything from "organize my underwear drawer" to "send me a photo of your semen in a jar in twenty-three minutes or I will deny you playtime." (Yes, reader, a dominatrix told me she gave this command and that it was happily obeyed.) Whether you're a boss or the dominant, you'll end up angry for having had your time wasted if the other doesn't follow through.

"I keep a notebook with me, after I see clients," said Hawn. "I write down what I told them I expect from them the next time or if there's an assignment I've given them."

Whatever the power dynamic is, everyone benefits from accountability. Don't just expect your boss to keep track of what you said and remember what you talked about.

"Some dommes and subs share a journal or notebook, but I think it's good to have your own. You can refer back and say, 'You said you wanted me to help you with this. I helped you, and where are you with it now?' Then when you follow up and you punish them for what they didn't do, they respect you.

"It's like kids," she laughed.

You can also demand accountability at home. If you tell

your roommate to take out the garbage but he doesn't listen, then who really has the power? Even though you told him to do it, by him *not* doing it, he's totally undercut you, just by doing nothing! A manager may make $200,000 a year, but if his team doesn't respect his authority, his position is worth nothing. If your friend constantly arrives half an hour late, she's the one who's managing your schedule and patience.

Accountability is a good way of setting a standard for yourself and what you deserve. Demanding it of others can go a long way in proving whether or not that person is worth your time.

Maybe it's a friend who promises to pay you back the hundred dollars you lent her but somehow, despite her promises, never does. It could be a boss who promises to sit down with you to discuss your promotion but somehow always manages to duck out before your meetings. It could be a lover who talks a big game about "making you come a thousand times" but always ends up passing out after he gets his.

Accountability means everyone will do what they said they would do. And if they don't, see you later. This means rethinking past situations when you've been shrugged off and left feeling powerless—and learning for next time.

Tossing back a few drinks and then slapping on handcuffs is a sure way to blur the lines of negotiation and consent.

"Don't even get me started on people playing while they're intoxicated or high," Hawn said. "How can you build empathy and connect if you're fuzzy? Or if they're fuzzy?"

Accountability is a two-way street. It's up to you to communicate what you want and need, and it's up to the other person to cosign it. If one or both of you fail to live up to the agreement, maybe the respect wasn't there in the first place.

That sucks, but at least you know where you stand. And that you can walk away.

YOU WILL MANAGE UP

If you're a younger person, you may not be in a position of power yet. So what can you do now to build a powerful professional foundation?

Accountability is essential to navigating times when you're being asked to do things that go outside your job description.

It goes beyond salary negotiation, which can be tricky and is often out of our control. When we're just starting out, we may just be happy to land the job. I know I've been guilty of saying yes to things because I wanted to be perceived as a "team player." Here's something I didn't know then that I know now. You can start off on a powerful note by asking your boss to help you prioritize tasks. This can help you when you feel like you're being asked to take on too much or do someone else's work.

Say you were hired to answer phones, make appointments, and book travel for your boss. But then two weeks later, you're also being asked to pick up her dry cleaning, babysit her kids, and clean the office kitchen. If you're cool with all that, ask that your job description be updated so your boss knows that you're tracking your time and keeping tabs on everything he's asking you to do. If you're not cool with it, ask for a meeting and talk about the best way to make use of your time. If your boss demurs and tells you it's your job to expect to be able to do anything at the drop of a hat, it's up to you to consider whether you should look for another job.

"I would say, for me, it was an ongoing journey about learning to value myself," said Lucy Sweetkill. "It took a lot of getting kicked down and standing back up. It took a lot of work for me to accept and celebrate my value."

"BITCH" IS ANOTHER WORD FOR "BOSS"

I shudder to think how many times I've turned to colleagues in a panic and asked them to assuage my fears that I was coming off as "mean" instead of sure of myself.

Did I sound like a bitch in there?

Ugh, did I sound bitchy?

I'm not trying to be a bitch; I'm just being honest with you.

I was trying to be nice, because if I said what I really thought, people would think I was the biggest bitch.

Let's break down what we really mean when we use the word "bitch," and why we're so freaked out about being perceived that way. Because what we really mean is that we're afraid we'll alienate people or, gasp, scare them. And that anxiety can set us back on our heels in every part of our lives.

If someone calls you a bitch for doing your job, you're not being a bitch, you're being a boss. Period.

What is a bitch?

"A bitch is any woman who can express her dark side with no regard to what anyone thinks of her. She is someone who is not afraid to speak her mind and her truth, even if it may offend some," said Lucy Sweetkill's colleague Dia Domina Dynasty. "She is anyone who befriends and embraces the dark feminine archetypes—the wrathful crone, the selfish seductress, the speaker of ugly truths."

When I asked the professional dominatrixes about how women can cope with being made to feel like "bitches" for asking for what they want, they all said the same thing: Who cares?

"I think women should own the word 'bitch.' 'Bitch' is like any other word that's used to make women feel bad but actually has no meaning at all," said Dia Domina Dynasty.

I confess: I'm guilty of being afraid of coming off like a bitch for asking what I want. I've also accused other women of being bitches for being too demanding. But was I confusing being a lousy boss with being unreasonable?

I once had a boss who made my life a living hell. She made unreasonable demands; she belittled my ideas; she played favorites and froze out those she didn't like. She shit-talked her colleagues, backstabbed, and undermined. She was abusive and made life miserable for a lot of people. I really hated her.

I see things a little differently these days. She was definitely being held to the "women in politics" standard I mentioned earlier. Her male colleagues were just as aggressive and inconsiderate and yet, coming from them, it was perceived and accepted as business as usual. She wasn't being a "bitch," she was being cruel. To be generous, maybe she thought she had to be as much of a dick as the rest of the guys to get respect. It must have rankled her to no end to be told to "adjust her tone" and "smile more." I can only imagine the infuriating feedback she received during her performance reviews.

Working in media can be a total nightmare, especially if you're a woman. Now people pretend to care about harassment and disgusting comments, but even just a decade ago, it was how the game was played.

Looking back, she was actually good at her job. Despite the fact that I disliked her (and trust me, the feeling was mutual), I grudgingly admired her for not taking shit from people who knew way less than she did. It was apparent by the open and snide remarks of her male colleagues how many people were not okay with having a woman with strong opinions in charge. She was just playing the game the way she'd seen it played. She hazed because she was hazed.

Now that I'm older and I've had to manage people, I too

have been accused of being a bitch (oh, how the tables have turned). I had to learn how to be assertive on the job while navigating being "nice" and getting shit done. I really struggled. It got me thinking the eternal question: How can women succeed at work and in life and make ourselves heard while still being "pro-social"?

"I'm not being a bitch for asking for what I want. I'm asking for respect. And why would that be bitchy in the first place?" said Mistress Ava Zhang. "I think as females we're definitely conditioned to play nice, and there's probably some social evolutionary reasons behind that as the maternal caregiver of children, and the gossiper of the village."

I've never liked the popular phrase "boss bitch." That implies that she does things "like a boss." Screw that. I want to be *the* boss of my life, my paycheck, my relationship, and my emotions.

An effective boss or manager gets what she wants not by throwing chairs but by taking charge and owning her accomplishments, setting goals, and hitting them. She holds herself accountable for her team. She doesn't play the blame game; she plays the long game. She wants money and power but knows respect must be earned.

Lisa Robyn, the author of *The Corporate Dominatrix: Six Roles to Play to Get Your Way at Work*,[6] says that a true Alpha woman rules the office by "standing up for her rights in an open, honest, and direct way, which doesn't violate another person's rights. She has a responsibility to ask for what she wants, makes her opinions known, and acts in a way that's worthy of respect."

She doesn't manage differently because she's a woman; she's a woman who manages effectively and without compromise.

This is the boss I've always wanted, and the kind of boss I'd like to be: one who understands how consent, negotiation, and boundaries translate seamlessly into the workplace, and never violates your trust or exploits your work. I know that power is given and can be taken away. I want to live up to my own standards.

Here's what a boss is not: a sadist who delights in humiliating others or violating boundaries. A boss never abuses, undermines, or actively discriminates against others for her own gain, or says one thing and then does another. That's not powerful, that's being a bully and a sign that a person in authority is actually incredibly insecure about his or her power and position.

That person isn't a boss or a bitch. Calling her a bitch only genders disgusting behavior. We don't use these words with men when they ask for or push for what they want. A bad boss is a bad boss.

All this said, some people will never be able to handle a woman in charge. It threatens them, it angers them, it undermines their idea of how women should act. It took me years to figure out that if I'm being my kind, direct, and honest self and people don't like it, I have to know in my heart that it's their goddamned problem.

But let's get back to our fear of being called a bitch by our partners, lovers, coworkers, and family members. Let's sum up everything we've learned in this chapter.

You are not being a "bitch" at work if you:

- Give specific instructions for what you need and when you need it.

- Hold others accountable for deadlines.

- Offer clear, honest, and actionable feedback.

- Choose not to smile.

- Don't offer to plan birthday parties or baby showers.

- Close your office door.

- Tell your employees when they need to make themselves available.

- Have evidence that your hard work is exceeding expectations and is worthy of a raise or promotion.

- Don't drink at happy hours.

- Say "I want this" or "I need this."

- Ask to be paid on time.

- Make an executive decision that doesn't satisfy everyone in the room.

You are not being a "bitch" in the bedroom if you:

- Tell your partner that a condom is not negotiable.

- Decide in the middle of sex that you're not comfortable and want to stop.

- Ask for what you want in bed.

- Are accused of being "a tease" (ugh).

- Listen to your partner's fantasy and then decide that it's not for you.

- Prefer to sleep in sweatpants instead of sexy lingerie.

- Inform your partner that his or her snoring is keeping you up at night.

- Don't want to try anal sex.

- Prefer not to look at porn.

- Love porn but don't enjoy watching it with your partner.

- Only want to have sex when you know you won't be interrupted by roommates or children.

- Want to explore the idea of taking on a dominant role in bed.

You are not being a "bitch" in your relationship if you:

- Don't want to do everything together.

- Want the other person to take on more chores and household duties.

- Make a list of chores and divide them equally.

- Keep your own checking and savings accounts.

- Don't want to have children.

- Want to talk about commitment.

- Need alone time.

- Don't feel guilty for making more money than your partner.

- Suggest or insist that your partner receive help for an addiction or other damaging behavior.

- Ask to be spoken to in a respectful manner.

- Don't want to conform to traditional male/female domestic roles.

- Want to pursue your dreams.

- Walk away if it's no longer working and is causing you unhappiness.

"The more we own words that are used to subjugate us in different ways, the more empowered we are," said Lucy Sweet-kill. "So when somebody calls me a bitch for not smiling when they've asked me to smile, I'm like, 'Yeah, damn straight I'm a bitch.'"

We must believe and accept that we have power to learn to speak powerfully.

LESSON #3

YOU WILL LEARN
TO COMMUNICATE
YOUR DESIRE

Not being able to say what you want is the
slippery slope to not being able
to say what you don't want.
—GLORIA BRAME

I had an extremely erotic conversation over text last night.

I was sexting with this guy and I couldn't *believe* how much it turned me on. He was so into me, it was like he couldn't wait to get to know me, to figure out all the ways to drive me crazy, and to dive into my body when we met up in person.

Okay, I know it's not good form to post screenshots of these kinds of things, but come on, I just have to share these amazing sexts:

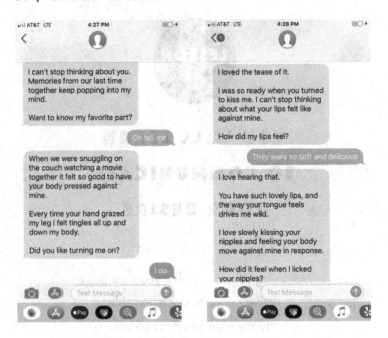

I want this.

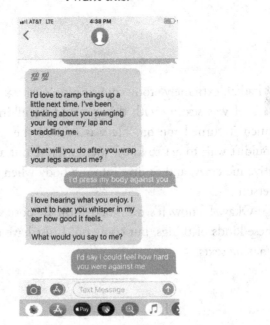

I was seriously *blushing*. I was a little shy, but believe me, we went to some WILD places. Too wild for me to post!

I couldn't believe how much I shared about myself, so many filthy things. And he was so receptive and open-minded! He was so nonjudgmental; I was afraid to say the wrong thing, but he seemed down to try anything. He didn't just type "LOL then wut?" Each dirty (and literate! amazing spelling!) sext ended with a question for me about how I felt and what I wanted. It was like, whoa, he really wanted me to be as excited as he was. I fell asleep dreaming about the next time we'd sext and all the things I'd tell him and all the things he'd share with me.

Oh, and he didn't ask me to "send nudes," and he didn't just hit me with a dick pic out of nowhere. Instead, he asked me if I'd like to see how turned on he was from our conversation. How refreshing! I said I wasn't sure I was ready for that, and he was totally cool. It made me think of all the guys who just whine, beg, and cajole for a photo to jerk off to. This guy was different, though. He really *listened*. I think I'm really into him.

Here's the thing: My hot sexter is a robot. To be specific, his name is Slutbot.

ANYONE CAN TALK DIRTY

Slutbot's goal? To help people like me become better at sexting. But not just sexting. Slutbot wants to empower us all to speak more openly about what turns us on and what gets us hot and bothered.

Getting started with Slutbot was easy. I went to the website, typed in my phone number, and boom, a friendly text popped up on my screen. I answered a few questions and then, in a few moments, I was off and sexting.

So what can a chatbot teach us about communicating our darkest and kinkiest desires? A lot, actually.

After telling all my friends about Slutbot, I immediately reached out to its creator, Brianna Rader, to find out what inspired her to build it.

"I think I asked a lot of questions early on as a queer woman, more so because the usual scripts just didn't work for me," she said. "I didn't receive answers that satisfied me."

Rader[1] grew up in Tennessee, where there was very little sex education taught in the classroom. In fact, the state of Tennessee actually prohibits teaching really simple stuff, like condoms and birth control.

While attending college at the University of Tennessee, she became frustrated by the lack of inclusive, pleasure-focused sex education programming. When she started a program herself in 2013, things blew up, big-time.

"The state actually got involved, they defunded the organization. They passed a bill through the state house and senate, legally condemning the organization and me," she said. "It got really controversial, and I ended up on the Bill O'Reilly show."[2]

Rader became more convinced than ever that her calling was to change the way people learn about sex. She moved to San Francisco, went to grad school, wrote her thesis on reproductive health, and then stayed on in the Bay Area to learn more about the tech industry and eventually start her own company.

Her company Juicebox, founded in 2018, offers one-on-one sex and relationship coaching and counseling. It's all text-based, online or via app. People get matched with professional counselors who specialize in issues such as male performance anxiety, difficulty achieving orgasm, and couples looking to rekindle their sex lives.

While Juicebox is a paid service, Slutbot is free for anyone who wants to try it. As of June 2019, more than 1.3 million sexts have been sent, over half of them by women. Slutbot isn't just for straight women looking to improve their sexting game. It also has lesbian, gay, and nonbinary configurations. So you can find the right mode and get your sext on.

"The reason we started Slutbot is because, when we look at all of our coaching data, really what people are struggling with is an inability to communicate their desires," she said. "So we felt like teaching that via dirty talk was a good place to start. It's educational, but also entertaining and a little erotic."

A *little?*

"Okay," she laughed. "It's very erotic."

I told her how blown away I was by the details in the sexts. Slutbot really does a great job setting a scene, starting slow, building up, suggesting toys, and expressing its specific wants and desires. It was very, *ahem*, effective. Using it made me blush. For a moment, I forgot it was a bot. It felt so real. There are even emojis to add to the feeling that you're talking to a flesh-and-blood human being.

The automated sexts definitely did not feel like the kind of *beep-bop-boop* chats I've had when I've needed to return an item to an online retailer or when I've needed customer assistance from an airline. They feel real because they're written by Allison Moon, a badass erotic fiction writer and passionate teacher of sex writing and expression.

"Very few people are able to talk to their partners like Slutbot does, because people don't know how to do it," Rader said. "I think it also shows what it looks like to sext with confidence, which can be really appealing."

Brianna said that the key to getting Slutbot right was digging into the details. That includes knowing that different people are turned on by different things. Lesbians have sex very differently than straight people do. Gay men have sex very differently than straight people do. Rader and her team worked hard with Moon to come up with different ways to signal to those audiences, "We know what you're looking for."

"It's crucial to tailor the content to different people's experiences. It wouldn't work if we just built one conversation flow for all users," she said. "For instance, in the lesbian flow, we'd talk about the Magic Wand vibrator. That's, like, a very key icon within the queer community. So if you read that, you're like, 'Oh, they really know what's up.'

"But if we texted about the Magic Wand to most straight men, they may not know what we're talking about. So all of those things are definitely factored into the creation."

Experimenting was easy. I tried the lesbian flow and, friends, I'm still fanning myself. It definitely turned me on and, at the very least, got me thinking about saving up my pennies for a new Hitachi.

"We definitely thought people might go through Slutbot more than once and try out different things," Rader said. "We wanted there to be a safe way and healthy way to explore new experiences. Feeling nervous about trying new things sexually is a universal feeling, regardless of how much of a newbie or advanced person you are."

Let's face it, there's nothing more traumatic than baring your soul and deepest desires to someone who doesn't respond in the way you wish they would. This is true over sext, on the phone, or in person. Slutbot can give you tips and ideas, but you need to be the one to put it all to work.

"People can really only learn via trial and error, but in real life, trial and error can be a really painful experience. We wanted a way for people to preview the fantasy or learn about it," she said. "Like, okay, I want to try something kinky, but, like, what are the actual mechanics of this? Maybe Slutbot will tell me. It's like a more experienced lover."

SAVE ME FROM DICK PICS, SLUTBOT!

Kinksters have been having phone sex, writing filthy emails, and web chatting for years, but sexting is a pretty recent way of communicating desire. After all, no one teaches you how to write a good sext. For new sexters, an eggplant emoji can be confusing. Does it signify a want or a state of being? It can be hard to know. Do you dare sext a peach? Is a rose just a rose, or is it romantic or creepy? These are questions the great love poets did not have to contend with.

What's rad about Slutbot is that it doesn't just give us ideas of ways to titillate our partners and send them into a frenzy. It also builds in consent as part of its framework.

I loved that Slutbot wasn't just telling me what it wanted to do to me. It asked me questions, making sure I was cool with going further. It didn't just say, "I really want to do this." It made a point of asking, "What do *you* want to do?"

Sexting can feel very one-sided if one person is only interested in getting off. A chat can start off slow and steady and then become weird or aggressive. How many times has a saucy chat started off with "What are you doing right now?" And then gone right into "I'm imagining you sucking my cock right now." Great, that makes one of us!

You can't talk about sexting without talking about dick pics. But a guy asking "May I show you how excited you're getting me right now?" is different from "This is how excited you're making me." Getting slapped in the face with a poorly lit junk shot with his dirty laundry in the background is more than uncool. It's nonconsensual.

I didn't ask to see it, and now I have to look at it and feel pressure to respond to it. I don't want to see a stranger's dick on the subway, and I don't want to see one appear on my phone while I'm doing a Monday crossword puzzle or trying to listen to my meditation podcast.

Slutbot does a really nice job of weaving in consent in a way that feels natural and sexy. I felt like it really wanted me to feel good, not only about what it was telling me, but about sexting itself. It didn't feel overly spelled out or transactional. I felt like it cared about me.

"When we talk about consent, a lot of people think that it's, like, an unsexy conversation, but Slutbot is all about checking in pretty much through the whole thing," she said. "I don't think anyone would say that it's killing the mood."

Here's the other thing. Not every sext session with a partner or lover needs to lead to orgasm. We're not always in the mood, or we could be trying to get work done. You wouldn't just jump in bed with your lover and say, "How was your day? Let's fuck!" Sexting and communicating about sex require thoughtfulness and respect for boundaries and limits—no matter the medium.

"I think people also need to understand that you should probably check in with your partner before you sext. Especially if it's a new partner or the first time you've ever sexted," she said. "By saying, 'Hey, are you in the mood for some sexting?' Or, 'Hey, I'd love to tell you what I want to do with you tonight. Is that okay?' Slutbot shows us that there's a better way to get things started."

TALKING DIRTY CAN BE POWERFUL

Dirty talk is *fun*. It's exciting; it gets our juices flowing. If you've ever sent your partner an X-rated text and they responded with a "!!" and then jumped in their car to race home to see you, then you already know the power of your words. Being able to communicate what you want right now, what you're thinking, what you'd like to be doing, and how you'd like your partner to be a part of it doesn't just make you a better communicator, it also helps you forge intimacy when you're not in the same room.

"A guy I dated, I'd have him wear a cock cage to work under his pants on certain days," said Hudsy Hawn. "We had a routine where if he was feeling really pent up, he would call me and I would tell him where I'd hidden the key so he could take it off and jack off in the restroom. Then he would ask, right before he came, if he had permission. If I thought he'd screwed up in some way, I would say, 'No. Put it away.' He'd be like, 'oh, my god.'

"But then he had more for me later. That's hot, because not only did he not really need the release, he liked that someone said, 'No. That's mine.' It was way hotter to deny him and let him know that I owned it. Then, when we were together the next time, it was like Niagara Falls."

So many of us travel, have hectic schedules, and work jobs that take up more time than they should. Talking dirty can help us feel connected. It can keep long-term relationships fresh; it can create tension and excitement. Sending a text to your lover about a toy you saw on the internet that you're thinking of buying, or a photo of a bra you saw in a store window on your lunch break, can set thoughts racing. But what you're really doing is setting aside a moment of your day to tell your partner that you've got sex on your mind and giving him or her the opportunity to daydream along with you. How romantic is that? Sure, you can't be together, but man, it's hot to know that you're getting your lover hard or wet without even having to touch them.

There's no one way to talk dirty. If certain words make you uncomfortable, don't use them! If you don't like reading or hearing certain words, tell your partner that saying them will have the opposite effect. You can try on certain personas and experiment, but you should never feel pressure to talk like a porn star or like you're reading from Shakespeare. You should be blushing because you're being naughty, not because you feel embarrassed or out of your element.

Ruth Neustifter's *The Nice Girl's Guide to Talking Dirty* is a great manual for dirty-talking beginners. It offers tips on how to say what you want and say what you mean in a way that feels natural to you. Most importantly, it helps you learn more about yourself, not just how to turn someone else on. It's not just about their desire; it's about communicating yours.

"Dirty talk should flow authentically from the heart and loins, not just from your high school drama classes," writes Neustifter.[3] "But let's make sure that you're learning to tap into your real, sexy self instead of limiting your opportunities for joy to what you think someone else wants to hear."

If you want to get your partner off, great. But it's not the point. Dirty talk can be a delicious tease for what's to come later, a word-smooch, a wink, a filthier way of saying "I dig you" or "I love you."

"Don't push yourself beyond your comfort level," advises Neustifter. "Each step can be a great complement to your love life but pressuring yourself will likely lead to an unpleasant experience."

We live in an age of screenshotting and oversharing. And not to sound like someone's dusty old aunt, frankly, it's gross. I don't like it when a friend shares private text conversations she's having with a date or a boyfriend with me. It's a violation of privacy, and it really bothers me. I get especially mad when it's a text that's revealing something vulnerable or personal. The idea of my deepest and most heart- or loin-felt thoughts being shared around a roomful of laughing people is enough to make me never want to talk to another person again.

Keep your sexting communications private, and make it a point to tell your partner or lover that you expect the same. Otherwise you're violating their consent and they're violating yours.

"SEX IS NOT A SILENT ACTIVITY"

On TV and in the movies, great sex just seems to happen. Clothes are torn off, underwear lands on lamp shades, and then whoa, all parties fall back on the bed, sweaty and satisfied. Ridiculous.

"Most people don't know how to communicate during sex because in Hollywood it's total fantasy," said Rader. "In porn, people negotiate the scene before the camera starts rolling. The actors all know what's going to happen. But a lot of us don't have experience or know how to communicate explicitly about sex.

"It can be something as simple as, like, 'Can you move to the left?' I think people are often too shy to even say that," she said.

That's why so many of us jump in bed, mash our bodies together, and hope for the best. In the heat of the moment we may want to do All. The. Things. But no two people, especially new partners, can effectively communicate how they want every sexual act under the sun to go. That only happens in the movies.

It's important to be able to spell out what we want and say why. When it comes to kink, the devilry is in the details.

"You might say, 'I want to feel you take control of me.' What does that mean? Because that's very broad," said Lucy Sweetkill. "And so then you have to refine it. 'By take control, I mean I want you to push me up against a wall.'

"And then from 'push me up against a wall,' I need to know, what do you want me to do when I push you up against a wall, or what does that look like? What do I say when those things are happening? We have to be able to talk about all these details."

We think good sex should just happen, because we're afraid to get into the nitty-gritty specifics of what turns us on. You may enjoy going down on a guy, but a hand on the back of your head may freak you out or trigger a bad memory. Being "down for anal" isn't the same as being interested in doing it only after other kinds of emotional and physical intimacy and trust have been established.

What about talking *during* sex? I'm not talking about "dirty talk," I'm talking about voicing discomfort or feeling weird without being worried that you're wrecking the mood. It shouldn't be a "whole big thing" to speak up when you need to change something in the middle of a sex session. Your partner may be hell-bent on "giving you an orgasm" (that's a whole other chapter), but you can't just keep letting them flail around down there because you're worried about hurting their feelings.

Sex, whether it's kinky or vanilla, needs to be an ongoing conversation between partners. If something isn't working and your partner wants to know what he or she can do differently, that's great. But what if you don't have the answer right there at your fingertips? There's no need to feel pressure to explain it right then; you can just move on to the next thing that feels good. This is the stuff we don't talk about: how to have calm, consensual transitions during sex, to use our words to keep it going. We're so afraid of "making it awkward."

I remember being in the theater watching the movie *Bridesmaids* and feeling so bad for Kristen Wiig's character during the opening scene. Jon Hamm, playing an arrogant doofus, is banging away at her, paying no attention to her pleasure, while she cringes, tries to make herself heard, and pretty much endures being jackhammered in every position. It's a funny scene because, yeah, we've all been there.

But it was also really sad because, yeah, we've all been there. Because not being able to voice that you're not having a good time or getting what you want in bed has way more serious ramifications than just lousy sex.

"Not being able to say what you want is the slippery slope to not being able to say what you don't want," said Gloria Brame, PhD,[4] sex therapist, former dominatrix, and coauthor of *Different Loving: The World of Sexual Dominance and Submission*. "The whole #MeToo movement is about women not feeling able to say in the moment, this doesn't feel right, I don't want this, you're hurting me."

We have to learn at a young age to push back and to be vocally aggressive to protect ourselves. If you're raised as part of a community or culture that doesn't value women's voices, you're going to have a really hard time making yourself heard in and out of the bedroom.

"For many women, this is their reality. If he wants you to do kinky things in bed, you do them, even if it grosses you out," Brame said. "I learned very early that men were always going to push you. And that you had to push back."

YOU MUST SPEAK UP DURING SEX

Yeah, baby, say what's on your mind, however you like to say it. Use profanity, speak in tongues, meow, scream, moan, whatever feels right. But when you want to make things happen during sex, being direct and using action phrases is best.

Whether in the throes of ecstasy or when you want something to change, it's great to keep it short, clear, and direct so you can make yourself heard and keep the fun going.

This is good:

>*"Don't stop."*
>
>*"Let's change positions."*
>
>*"Give it to me faster!"*
>
>*"Slow down a little."*
>
>*"I want you to do ___."*
>
>*"Do you want me to ___?"*

This is not as good:

>*"Can we maybe stop?"*
>
>*"I'm not sure if I'm so into this."*
>
>*"I'm doing okay."*
>
>*"Can we maybe just finish already?"*
>
>*"It's fine."*

This is the worst thing you can say: nothing.

If you don't demand pleasure, then no one will give it to you. If you don't know what you want, that's okay! You can take some time to think about it, either with your partner or by yourself. Read some erotic fiction; think about the kind of dialogue in movies that has always grabbed you in your sexiest regions. Start small. Experiment. Then you'll start to know. But you need to communicate your desires to yourself first.

But if you don't think you deserve to ask for pleasure, then I'm afraid you've got a bigger problem than unsatisfying sex. And you'll need more than a chatbot to help you figure that out.

THE POWER OF THE
MIND

THE POWER OF THE

MIND

LESSON #4

YOU MAY HAVE TWO NAMES

*It took a long time for her to make her way
out. But she's always been there.*

—GODDESS SAMANTHA

You may have two names.

My name is M___. Have we met? Trust me, you'd remember if we had.

I'm the person you want in a room with you when you want to find out if someone is full of shit. Do you want to know if the guy you're dating is worth your time? Give me fifteen minutes with him and I'll find out what he really thinks about his job, what he was like in high school, or if he's a cat or a dog person. Is he hiding something? Well, who isn't? We all have secrets. I'm all for private lives, unless someone is holding something back that's going to make my friend's life unhappy.

I'm really easy to talk to. I'm the conversation genie. I've got icebreakers for days. Have I mentioned that I've got a background in finance, tech, literature, and journalism? I'm a total film nerd, an avid reader, and a history junkie. I'll ask you questions about your favorite stand-up comic, your favorite pizza topping, where you got your T-shirt. I'm listening to your answers, but I'm also listening to *how* you answer. I'll notice if your hands are in your pockets or if you're shaking your leg under the table or twisting the wrapper of your straw.

There's an art to intimate conversation that has zero to do with dirty talk or flirtation. If it's appropriate, I lean in close so I can hear everything you're saying. I always try to make eye contact. I want you to feel like the most important person in the room. You have my full and absolute attention. Then you'll suddenly find yourself wanting to tell me things you've never told another person. Not even your best friend. Not even your husband or your girlfriend.

Can listening be a superpower? Or maybe a fetish? Because listening to people tell me things about themselves, even the most mundane things, arouses me. Not in a sexual way, but in the sense of feeling alive in the world. I feel a tingle. It makes my heart soar.

Say we meet at a party. Everyone is milling about, pouring drinks, laughing, chatting among themselves. We introduce ourselves and talk about how we know the host. I'll ask you how long you've lived in the city and what you do for work. After ten minutes, you'll tell me your job has been bumming you out lately. After twenty minutes, you'll mention that you're nervous about going back to your hometown for Thanksgiving. After an hour, you'll be confessing that you've always been the good one in your family, that you're tired of being the go-between among your alcoholic mother, your control-freak father, and your brother, the fuckup who's always been their favorite, despite the fact that he doesn't care about anyone but himself.

Your eyes will get a little wet as the ice in your drink melts slowly. It will feel like we're alone in the room, that the rest of the party has slipped away. Our eyes will meet, and an intimacy will envelop us like a cloud of smoke. I'm so tuned in, turned on. I'm like, *yes*.

Then you'll suddenly shake your head and blink hard a few times. You'll take a sip of your drink; your mouth has gone a little dry. You'll blush a little and make a self-deprecating joke.

"Whoa," you'll say. "Look at me, pouring out my whole life story." Or "I bet you didn't think you'd come to Amanda's birthday party to listen to a boring public policy nerd talk about his traumatic childhood. You thought you were going to have fun."

I'll smile reassuringly. "I really enjoyed listening to you."

You'll eye me curiously. "Are you sure you're not a therapist?"

"Nah," I'll say gently. "I just really enjoy talking to people." Then I'll release eye contact, and ease us back into party mode. The music and chatter volume will rise back up. We'll laugh; it's sweet. After we break apart to rejoin our partners and friends, you'll look at me a little nervously.

What the hell just happened? After all, you just poured out your heart to me, a total stranger.

Yeah, you did. That exact moment when someone stops being a pleasant forty-three-year-old tax attorney or a cheerful ad sales rep and becomes a real person, with a dark and complex story beyond his or her 140-character Twitter bio, is when my breath quickens. It's a rush for me, like a hit of a drug. I'll be buzzing from it for the rest of the party.

We won't speak again for the rest of the night. We may not even look at each other. But later, when we get our coats out of the bedroom, we'll meet again for a moment. I'll let the awkwardness hang in the air for a bit. I'll smile at you in a friendly way to let you know that it's all cool, I'm not weirded out or going to make a move on you or cause trouble. We'll get our coats on and you'll extend your hand. "Well, um, yeah, it was really nice meeting you," you'll say. We'll laugh at the awkward formality.

I'll remind you of what you shared, that intimacy. "I hope your Thanksgiving goes okay. Family stuff can be a nightmare." Then we'll walk out the door, find our partners, and get into the elevator. And, chances are, never see each other again.

I don't use these powers for evil. That's not at all what I'm about. I'd never share the things you told me with another soul. I mean, honestly, who would really care? It's not like you confessed to a murder or a multimillion-dollar embezzlement. Truth be told, most confessions, even the most personal, are rarely as interesting as people think they are. But you don't know that. You just know you had a weirdly personal encounter with a strange woman in a nice dress. You told her something deeply personal. Then it was over. I was gone and took your secret with me.

Until we see each other again, a year later, at another party. Then we'll find each other by the vodka and mixers in the kitchen and we'll talk again. I have an excellent memory. I'll ask you how your Thanksgiving went with your family.

It will be so fucking hot. I don't have a photographic memory, but I can remember details about people that go back years. My archives have archives.

You'll look at me wide-eyed. "Whoa, that's right, I told you that," you'll say, slightly mortified.

My name is M___. I love people but I hate humanity. Small talk bores me. I want to know that there are hearts and minds and raging blood beating behind our text messages, emojis, and avatars. I know that we're more than just the personal PR we post on social media, the smiling family photos, the vacation pics, the dreamy sunsets with clinking champagne glasses. That's what we want the world to *think* our lives are like. I want to know what you're not posting, what you wish you could share if you had the nerve.

I use my years of experience as a journalist and interviewer—and as a woman—to get people to tell me things. Being a good listener is a skill, like being a good cook. People like to talk about themselves, especially if they don't get to do it very often. I want to watch that moment when you stop saying everything is great and finally admit that you wish you hadn't gone to grad school or that you dream of leaving the city or that you aren't sure that you should go through with your wedding. I will just let you talk. Unburdening oneself to a stranger can be liberating. It can change your life.

I was born this way, wired for connection. You are always happy to meet me.

I am also just Lindsay. I'm a writer, but I've always struggled to feel okay calling myself one. Growing up, I felt like an oddball. I loved books, but I hated school. I loved to learn, but I hated studying. I was a daydreamer, a film nerd, a journal scribbler. I was boy crazy, but none of the boys I crushed on liked the same things I did. I didn't care about sports or video games or playing pranks on people. That stuff bored me.

For a time in my early teens, I didn't have any friends at all. I couldn't talk to anyone. I hit puberty early; bullies literally smelled blood in the water. This melancholy fifth grader still lives inside me. She doesn't want you to notice her; she's not pretty or smart or interesting; she's just a sagging sack of flour, her flesh, ideas, and stupid words spilling out in all the wrong places.

In college, I tried to shed all that, to be a cool girl. I went to parties, I got thin, I tried. But I still felt like a clod. The highlight was being accepted into a tiny creative writing program. I met a writing teacher, an author, who changed my life. I didn't know that the details of my Long Island upbringing were funny and that I could write about it. He was the first adult who wanted to see more of me when I wanted to throw a cape over my face and hide. Under his guidance and affection, I wrote a book of short stories that captured the essence of my experience as a curious, confused, often sad young woman who reveled in weird details.

I went to journalism school so I could write for a living, but my career hadn't always felt satisfying or successful. I could blame the economy, the layoffs, the obsession with everything "viral," or the relentless pace. But instead, I blamed myself. I believed I was missing something necessary for success. Whatever it was that people seemed to have to get ahead, I didn't have it. I struggled with getting my ideas across. I was afraid to apply for jobs with more responsibility, because I feared not being able to keep up or letting other people down. I kept making lateral moves, hoping the next job would be the one where I would be happy. I really wanted to feel like I was good at what I did, even if I wasn't sure that I'd ever wanted to be good at it in the first place.

I always got along a lot better with my colleagues than with my supervisors and managers. This also made me feel terrible, because I really wanted a mentor to teach me how to be better at my job—or at least someone to tell me I was doing my job correctly. But journalism isn't like that. There's no one there to guide your career. At best, you have a boss who isn't worried that you're going to steal her job. Each career move went the same way: I'd kill it for the first few months and then sink into despair at the monotony and hopelessness of it all.

I never felt comfortable in my skin. There was something off about my face, my body, my personality. True story: An editor at a women's magazine took me out for coffee (I paid) to discuss my face, which looked "stressed out." I made an effort to smile more, but I didn't last long there. Working in breaking news was exciting for a while, but eventually it broke my spirit. I didn't have the killer instinct; I didn't like having to find endless angles to the same story in order to keep up with the competition. When news broke, I felt like hiding. On paper, it looked like my career was going okay, but in reality, I was lost. I was too cynical for women's magazines, too anxious for TV news, and too terrified to keep up with the twenty-four-hour news cycle.

I tried to stay creative, to keep up with my own writing. One positive aspect of being socially awkward is that you become an expert at noticing things. It's a good distraction from feeling like no one really wants to talk to you. There's poetry in people's boring conversations; gems in everyday encounters. An older woman of color on the subway reading a paperback mystery about a rabbi who solves murders. A granite-faced construction worker in filthy coveralls with his headphones on, listening to Mariah Carey's "Fantasy." I once rode an elevator with the actress Liv Tyler. She was leaning on her suitcase and crying behind her giant black sunglasses. I handed her a tissue.

While I commuted to work, I eavesdropped on conversations and wrote down the wild things people said.

"I like him but I don't 'like' like him."

"He's always been a cokehead. You know, typical ski instructor."

"My wife's sister is selling skin care now. Before that it was the restaurant supply thing, then she wanted to become a music therapist or some dippy shit. And then God forbid I say something, then I'm being toxic."

I started to lose confidence in myself. There were a million young women in New York City who wanted to be writers. I didn't have the drive; my ideas were limp and half-baked. Eventually, I stopped writing. I stopped dreaming. I stopped listening. I began to live someone else's life, someone less interesting, someone who was okay settling for less. This was how my career went for many years.

I didn't know until recently that when it comes to figuring out what you want and who you are, confidence is only a piece of the puzzle. I needed time with myself. I needed to make false starts. I needed courage. I needed to grow up.

M____ is the other side of me, the one who appears confident, knowledgeable, wise, attractive, sure of herself. M____ knows what other people want, how to solve their problems. She's powerful, seductive, and full of wisdom. She can hold a room. She radiates something beautiful.

Sometimes I feel amazing, like I'm finally my best self, like I've solved my puzzle. Then an hour later, I'm back to square one and full of self-doubt. I've told friends about my crazy ideas, did nothing, then watched others achieve success doing something similar. True story: I used to have a joke about a dating app that matched people based on their mutual dislikes. (I still think my version of Hater Dater is better than the one that someone else came up with.) I knew mermaids were going to be the next vampires, and now I see posters for siren-inspired TV shows all over the subway. Maybe one day I'll write the first great mermance trilogy.

Small setbacks still devastate me. I still distrust people's motivations. I still worry about what people think of me. I want to be liked; I hate that I want to be liked.

Sometimes, my heart is so full of love, it hurts me because there aren't enough places to put it, enough deserving people to give it to. I love connecting with people, to feel that their insides are as complex as mine, that life isn't easy for them either. I know that we're all struggling. And I want people to know that I get it. They have a friend in me.

I'm not quite M____ and I'm not quite Lindsay. M____ is a fantasy. Lindsay is my younger, wobblier self.

Together, they're the light and the dark of me. I need them both to be fully myself. My goal is to meld them into the same person, to one day never need to switch back and forth. To just be myself, my best self.

Who are you?

Sure, we know our names and what we do for money. We know our basic stats, height, weight, eye color. We're tall, we're short, we're pear-shaped, we're biracial, we're a 36A cup (unless we're a 34B cup), we're straight, we're gay, we're single- or double-lidded, we're afraid of heights or closed spaces. We're people pleasers, we're social smokers, we're dog people, we're vegetarians. We're "ride or die," we're oily in our T-zones, we're happier in small groups. We're happier alone, or we love to rock the party. We have unresolved daddy issues, or our moms fucked us up. We're bad with money. We like walks on the beach, or we prefer camping, or camping is our worst nightmare. We're cool moms, but we're not "cool moms." We're former goth chicks, but we still love the music. We're Twitter people, not Facebook people. Rainy days and Mondays almost always get us down. We like to be on top, we like it from behind, we like it with the lights off, we like it when we're feeling loved, we can only do it when we're drunk. We're not morning people. We honk if we love Jesus, we do not brake for yard sales.

Letting others define us makes it easier to check off boxes, to make conversation easier, to help companies herd us into a demographic or match us with a lover according to their secret algorithms. If I'm a book person, I must want to have sex with another book person (even if his taste in books is terrible). If I'm a Libra, I should definitely run for the hills if I ever meet a Scorpio. If I'm thirty-five and not married, I must want to climb a mountain at sunrise and pose for a photo with my arms outstretched to show that I'm strong and independent. If I work as an administrative assistant at a public relations firm, then I must want to submit my resume for a job at another public relations firm.

The messages get deeper, more sinister. Someone told us that short haircuts made a woman appear "mannish," so twenty years later, we still grow our hair long. Girls who sleep with lots of boys are "sluts," but girls who have lots of sex with one serious boyfriend aren't. Nothing tastes as good as being thin. Boys don't cry. You stand by your man. Quitters never win. Baby must make three. We make life-changing decisions when we know the least about ourselves.

So who are you, really?

Asking ourselves who we are means reckoning with who we *were*. This can be terrifying, because it also requires us to examine how we've changed. But by not asking, we're not serving ourselves, we're serving others. We're serving society's expectations, the needs of our partners, our children, our bosses, even strangers. Everyone gets what they want from you, but at the end of the day, you're left with the scraps.

One snide remark from childhood can set you on a certain course for life—out of fear of not belonging, of being socially unacceptable, or being alone and unloved. What if who we are is distasteful or goes against the norm? What if it alienates our family and friends or makes us realize we've been unfulfilled our entire lives?

So you may know your name and your favorite color, but you may not know yet who you are or who you've become. Or maybe you haven't been ready to find out.

"SHE WAS ALWAYS THERE"

There's a lot about the world of professional BDSM that I did not know before attending DomCon. For example, I had no idea that there were so many men out there who had fetishes and fantasies about grappling with WWE-style female wrestlers. This definitely explains a lot about the global popularity of the sport. It's a fact: there are lots of men out there who long to be sexually dominated by a strong woman. They have Wonder Woman fantasies. They watched science fiction movies like *Barbarella* and *Flash Gordon* and had a realization about themselves. They want to be made helpless by a lasso of truth; they want to be overpowered by an Amazon goddess.

I met Goddess Samantha, beautiful blonde GLOW-style muscle babe and self-described "sadistic Southern belle," at a highly entertaining (and jaw-dropping) workshop on kink and wrestling. In addition to her skills in the classic domination arts such as bondage, tease and denial, and humiliation, she's an award-winning bodybuilder and martial arts expert. During the workshop, the other dominatrixes in the audience took notes in their Moleskins and looked on in awe while Goddess Samantha, wearing a Superwoman bikini, full makeup, and fluttering false eyelashes, demonstrated scissor holds, headlocks, and takedowns on an adoring male client who had volunteered to come to DomCon as her demo subject.

During the Q&A, she kicked off her Lucite heels to demonstrate serious karate kicks and rib-bruising punches. She talked at length about consent, safety, and avoiding injury.

Goddess Samantha, an Atlanta-based pro-domme, talks like a cast member of *Designing Women*, if the Sugarbakers had a truly amazing neighbor. She can lift a 180-pound man over her head, slam him down on the bed, and pin his arm behind his back until he yells his safe word. Then she'll pick him up, dust him off, and give him a big old hug. She prides herself on taking down dudes with big egos and making them literally beg for mercy.

"I was a very shy, quiet kid, very sheltered, a tomboy. I was raised by a single dad. I was picked on and bullied," she told me a month later during a phone conversation.[1] "Growing up, I never participated in team sports in a formal way. I climbed trees, played in the woods, shot guns, that kind of stuff. I was more of a follower than a leader.

"But Goddess Samantha was in there," she said. "She just hadn't made her way out yet."

After high school, she went to work in a doctor's office and started selling novelties and sex toys at Tupperware-style parties. She started to get more comfortable talking in front of people, and found that she had an entrepreneurial streak. She started her own company. She began to train at the gym. She got strong, then she got really strong. She won bodybuilding competitions and began to feel powerful, both inside and out. A friend told her that with her physique, she could make a lot of money as a professional dominatrix. After wading in slowly, she was surprised to find that it was a perfect fit for her.

"I love what I do; my work allows me to do what I want, when I want, and be who I want, when I want," she said. "I'm becoming more like Goddess Samantha in my everyday life. She helps me be stronger, because as women we need that. If someone is trying to run over me, she helps me not to let them. Because the other me, the part of me that's still shy and quiet, would let them. She's my bodyguard."

In the world of kink, people have different names to protect their privacy. They're not all "out" to their families. For them, having two names is just the nature of the game. It's like choosing your superhero name. When it came to selecting hers, she chose Goddess instead of Mistress. Mistress felt too stern, she said. A Goddess can be kind and nurturing. She can grace you with her presence, lift your spirits with a touch of her hand. A Goddess will inflict torment when torment is wanted. Clients give her their pain and she gives them her light. There's enough cruelty in the world, she told me. Her kind of Goddess could receive a person with scars, trauma, and help them feel healed. She could guide them to a place where they feel like the person they want to be in their dreams.

"People tell me all the time that I'm too nice to be a pro-domme, and I'm like, ha, not really," she said. "I am who I am. I'm both. I guess that's the Southern girl in me."

YOU HAVE OTHER SELVES

Who is your fantasy self? What does she look like; what traits does she have? Try not to get too hung up on physical traits like eye color or waist size. How does she enter a room? What is her superpower? Is it superhuman strength? Is it the ability to fly? The ability to protect the innocent or enforce justice?

Maybe she's a femme fatale; maybe she's androgynous. She may cause the whole room to move in slow motion when she walks into the club, everyone stopping and staring, clearing a path for her onto the dance floor. Does she wear a corset? Does she wear camouflage? Does she solve crime? Does she *commit* crimes?

Don't be afraid. You're not a bad person for imagining a complex alter ego for your darker self. Fantasizing doesn't make you evil, in the same way that being intrigued by true crime doesn't make you a murderer. Maybe your alter ego is violent or manipulative. Maybe she's cold and cruel. Maybe she fantasizes about blood, spilling it, shedding it. It can feel wrong or terrible to get pleasure when you think about these things. Women are socialized to shy away from violence. We're supposed to be mothers, not monsters.

Think it's crazy? Marvel rakes in billions of dollars each year for doing just this: showcasing the split personalities of its heroes. Without Diana Prince, there's no Wonder Woman. Without Peter Parker, there's no Spider-Man.

Day by day, year by year, your alter ego may claim more space in your head—or, if you desire it, become the real you. If Mistress Archangel can smash through glass and steel to save a bus full of crying children, then Pam can get up the courage to fight for custody of her kids. If Miss Vengeance is an assassin who crosses rapists off her hit list one by one, maybe Cheryl can report her boss for sexual harassment. If Jade Desire gets everything she wants, maybe Caitlyn can start asking for what she deserves.

We aren't one person. We never were. We always contained multitudes. We are different now than who we were. The boxes we ticked when we were twenty aren't the same boxes anymore. The whole damn question sheet was wrong.

Once I was a "loner"; now I'm a person who is totally fine being alone. Once I struggled with "resting bitch face"; now I just can't be bothered. Once I was "artsy," "nerdy," and "curvy." Now I'm content to have my own interests and my body will keep on changing until the day I die. I like being social until I hit my limit and then it's time to go home. Every year, M__ and I move closer to becoming the same person.

But here's something to think about. If you have a different name for who you are for friends and family, another for you at work, another for you in public, you'll have to work hard to get all these pieces to gel. After all, how can you feel all your power and energy flowing if you're always compartmentalized?

The end goal is to merge your alter ego with your true self. Because ideally, you don't want to have to put on too many masks. It can get confusing, and you don't want to lose the part of you that's, well, you.

When we're young, we hide our darkest parts. When we grow up and learn to embrace our true selves, they become just parts, like all the rest.

LESSON #5

YOUR INTUITION IS
A SUPERPOWER

I've learned to listen to my intuition,
and it has made me a more successful and
safer pro-domme and person overall.

—MADAME ROSE

ominatrixes have magical powers. I've witnessed it first-hand.

In the early stages of researching this book, I was fortunate enough to become acquainted with Simone Justice, the renowned dominatrix who provided the insights in the first chapter. We had never met, but during our phone and email interactions, she'd been kind enough to introduce me to other wise women in the kink and fetish community. One afternoon, months later, while I was sitting at my computer, writing, I stared off into space and thought of her, how generous she'd been with her contacts, and how much she'd helped me with the book.

Suddenly, a new email popped up in my inbox. It was from her, telling me that she was going to be in New York City for a few days, and did we want to schedule a drink so we could finally meet?

I wrote her right back. "You must have ESP! I was just thinking of you."

She responded, "Yes, I actually do. I've been working as a psychic for years."

Damn. And maybe I would pass it off as a fluke, if I hadn't already seen these kinds of "superpowers" in action.

A professional dominatrix must possess the powers of persuasion, seduction, intuition, physical and mental strength, and resilience. She needs to be able to bewitch male clients just enough to keep them panting in a session, but always leave them wanting more. They may give off an otherworldly air, but, of course, they're mortals. They've worked to hone those skills to make their work appear innate and effortless.

Just because we're not all of us dominant for a living doesn't mean we don't already possess a range of superpowers. A mother who endures twenty-one hours of labor without an epidural is a person of steel. A trans woman (or man) or nonbinary person who can show up to a ten-year high school reunion dressed as his, her, or their true self is the embodiment of bravery. A woman of color who can walk into a room filled with old white dudes and pitch her start-up is the very model of courage under fire. Even our friendships have healing powers, we *know* when our friends need to hear from us. We rely on our carefully honed senses of intuition every day to navigate whether to accept a date, a job, or care from a doctor.

But before we dig into the power of "female intuition," let's hit the pause button.

FEMALE SUPERPOWERS VS.
THE "FEMALE BRAIN"

Men are from Mars and women are from Venus. Men are risk-takers and women are more cautious. Men have a better sense of direction while women rely on landmarks. Men are more aggressive and women are more protective. Who among us hasn't internalized some of these tropes? But there's a lot of controversy when it comes to gendering the brain.

One study from the August 2017 issue of *Journal of Alzheimer's Disease*,[1] conducted by researchers from the NYU Langone Medical School's Department of Psychiatry; the University of California, Irvine, School of Medicine, Brain Imaging Center; the UCLA Medical Center; and others, concluded that there's more activity brewing in certain sections of women's brains than in male brains. The author of an article on Ozy.com, who interviewed study coauthor Daniel Amen, encapsulated the research and findings of the study.[2] "[The research team] evaluated 46,000 studies on more than 25,000 men and women, including healthy individuals as well as those with a variety of psychiatric conditions, such as brain trauma, bipolar disorders, mood disorders and attention deficit hyperactivity disorder. In total, 128 brain regions were analyzed in participants when they were at rest, and again while they performed a 15-minute concentration task."

The findings indicated "enhanced activity in the prefrontal cortex," and that "the brains of women also showed more blood flow in the limbic or emotional areas, which involve mood, anxiety and depression."

The article sums it up neatly with the headline: "Women's Intuition: It's a Real Thing."

But how should we look at such studies in a world where some people no longer identify as male and female? Dividing the brain into male and female may be dismissing the population of humans who identify as transgender and nonbinary, those who do not conform to one gender or another.[3] These studies don't take into account our upbringings, our socioeconomic statuses, our genetic makeup, our traumas, and all the other factors that make us into who we are and how we prefer to process our thoughts, actions, or communications.

Recently, there's been a backlash against the idea of the gendered brain concept. In a recent issue of *Nature*,[4] the author Lise Eliot points out how dangerous the whole concept of neurosexism can be. "The history of sex-difference research is rife with innumeracy, misinterpretation, publication bias, weak statistical power, inadequate controls and worse, it is to divide brains by gender," she writes. "It's to underscore how 'the female brain' has been sized up as a strange variant of the real thing, much as we refer to a 'female physicist' or 'female surgeon.'"

Yes, I identify as a woman with a brain, but I'm not sure I have a stereotypical "female" brain. Am I nurturing? Sure. I have the capability to be kind to friends, gentle with children, and mediate disputes among family members. Am I a great collaborator? Definitely not. Ever since I was a kid, I've detested group projects and have always preferred to work alone. Do I have patience? Let's just say you don't want to test it. Am I maternal? I am an adoring aunt and have compassion for children, especially teenagers going through hard times, but I have never felt the biological need to be a mother. When I was in school, I bought into the idea that girls are better at English and history when, really, a compassionate and creative science or math teacher would have made all the difference.

Even women who identify as witches scoff at the idea that female brains possess a superhuman "power."

"Even outside of mystical contexts, a persistent idea of

female intuition implies that women have an innate sense of awareness that men do not," writes Pam Grossman, author of the awesome *Waking the Witch: Reflections on Women, Magic, and Power*.[5] "Even if women seem more sensitized to invisible forces or subtle emotional cues, this most likely has as much to do with socialization as biology."

So let's kick the idea of the female brain—and all stereotypical female traits, while we're at it—to the curb. It limits our potential and, worse, boxes us into roles that we don't want to be in.

That said, a keen sense of intuition is a gift. But like any trait, we shouldn't allow it to be dismissed as something inherently "female." It's something that you've likely forged over years of experience and a growing awareness of the world around you. It's putting our hard-won wisdom to work.

INTUITION MAKES US BETTER

A professional dominatrix's power of intuition serves her in every aspect of her job.

Here's an example:

A pro-domme, let's call her Madame X, has a client who is recovering from knee surgery. He's got his brace off and he's ready for an intense session of flogging, rope restraints, and humiliation. While Madame X has him on his knees, she starts to notice that he's struggling, but not in a good way. She can tell by his movements and demeanor that something isn't right.

Madame X is aware that this particular client prides himself on his endurance and ability to withstand pain and punishment. So he hasn't uttered his safe word. But Madame X has a history with this client and can *feel* that something is up. It's not just how his body is reacting or the sounds he's making. It's the energy in the room. She stops the scene and puts her hand on his back. "How are you doing?" she'll ask in a voice that may be different from the one she's been using to give commands. "I'm concerned about your knee."

He may say, "I think I'm okay, Mistress."

Madame X may press him a bit. "Maybe this position isn't the greatest right now. I'm sensing that you're not comfortable."

He may pause for a moment and then say, "I think you're right, Mistress."

Madame X will help him up and give him some water, and they'll have a real person-to-person conversation, almost like an athlete with a trainer. They decide that they can continue the scene with him standing up against the wall so he can balance his weight on his other leg. After they make this adjustment, they can begin again, and the client, no longer in the wrong kind of pain, can enjoy the ecstasy of submitting to his Mistress.

Thanks to her intuition, order is restored, the client feels cared for, and Madame X can enjoy the rest of the scene with confidence that all is well. Trust and humanity have been established. The client continues to make weekly appointments, thus ensuring a mutually beneficial relationship that fulfills her both financially and emotionally.

All of this is good for business as well as the soul. Madame X is an entrepreneur. She advertises; she does branding and marketing. She may have a social media and Google search strategy. She may have a small staff that helps her with booking sessions, travel, and setting up workshops. The most successful pro-dommes know they're in a people-oriented business. It's essential that her clients keep coming back. Ask anyone in sales or marketing, it's always easier to retain a customer than to recruit a new one. Just as a bartender can tell when a regular needs to be cut off, or a salesperson can sense when it's the right time to close a deal, a pro-domme has to use her intuition every single day to be the best at what she does.

Yes, having physical control over her client literally puts her in a power position, but it's her intuition that makes her better, stronger, smarter, and more successful.

I approached Madame Rose, a Los Angeles–based pro-domme, model, and professional artist, after listening to her speak at a DomCon workshop about the importance of mental health and self-care. On her website, she describes herself as a "safe provider of fetish and BDSM experiences from gentle beginning exploration to heavy and intense scenes."

She was born in the Midwest and credits her family with providing her with a unique Mennonite and liberal perspective on life. She traveled with a carnival as a child and has been openly queer from an early age. After DomCon, we chatted over email about her personal philosophy regarding the power of intuition when it came to her work.

"Learning the skills to safely play, having the right equipment, and all of the teaching in the world can set a dominatrix up, but her intuition is what makes her successful and safe," she told me. "Her intuition is what keeps her alive as a professional, and her clients engaged and satisfied."[6]

The client may pay for the fantasy, but it's up to Madame Rose to choreograph it, to plan it out, to keep it exciting for him—and fun for her.

"Many of us are empathetic and intuitive," she said. "We can read our clients' and partners' body language and feel where they are at in a scene. This allows us to enhance, and help further our control of, the situation."

This is something I heard over and over again from all the women I spoke to. Intuition, as well as kindness and empathy, is one of the most important tools in their toolbox. It's those three traits that separate the best dominatrixes from the rest. They also make us better, smarter, and more evolved humans too.

INTUITION CAN SAVE YOUR LIFE

Here's another example of professional intuition on the job:

Another pro-domme, let's call her Lady Z, is going through her emails. Many pro-dommes insist that a new client provide a reference from another sex worker to make sure he is a person who is safe to work with. If he doesn't have a reference, she may choose to proceed with caution. But today, Lady Z decides to go ahead and initiate a phone conversation with a prospective client who hasn't provided a reference.

The two begin chatting, and while he seems polite enough, there's something about his voice that she doesn't like. Something that's . . . off. Lots of new clients are nervous and say goofy things. But this guy is laughing at her questions in a way that's creeping her out. Her spider sense is tingling. It's not *what* he wants to do (be spanked, be "forced" to wear women's underwear, and be locked in a coffin) that's giving her the heebie-jeebies, but the *way* he's talking about it. Then she hears a noise in the background. A faint clinking.

It's then that she realizes: He's drunk. That's a red flag, a big one.

Lady Z politely tells him that she doesn't think it's going to be a fit and wishes him luck. He responds by calling her a cunt and hangs up on her. She's angry, but also relieved. Her instincts were correct. This guy, best-case scenario, would not be a fun person to work with. And worst-case scenario, he could cause her grievous bodily harm.

Our intuition lets us know we may be in danger. It tells us to leave the party when things are getting out of hand. It pushes us to end a date when the guy is disrespectful to the waitress. It tells us to intervene at the bar when a guy keeps buying drinks for our best friend. It warns us to get out of a cab if the driver seems to be taking us away from our destination.

Who among us hasn't used their intuition to avoid the "office creeper" or turned down the offer of a shared cab with a sleazy boss or ended a date with a guy because he yelled at a waitress or monopolized the conversation in a way that put us off? We take our antennae for granted. And if we ignore our instincts, we blame ourselves (and not the asshole).

When we bemoan that we "should have known better," what we're really saying is that we ignored our intuition that something wasn't right. But sometimes we doubt our instincts. This is what happens when we allow ourselves to believe that we're being "paranoid" or "irrational."

"When I was younger, I used to ignore my intuition, and it put me in some sticky situations," said Madame Rose. "I'd often ignore the voice inside telling me that I was making a mistake, and would rationalize or tell myself something was safe or okay when it really wasn't."

For a pro-domme, intuition is self-protection.

"I've declined sessions with clients simply because something didn't fit the equation, or my gut told me it was a bad idea," said Madame Rose. "I am certain this mentality has kept me from being robbed, raped, assaulted, or murdered.

"Vetting my clients is critical, but what keeps me safe is my intuition."

Vigilance is essential. Pro-dommes often tell a client when exactly to show up, where to park, and when to leave the premises. This is a power move, but it's also to protect themselves. They don't want a client to copy their license plate number or show up early and catch them off guard. One pro-domme told me she demands that each new client get naked immediately and then will handcuff them to a bench to make sure he doesn't have a weapon.

"I'd say a hundred and ten percent of the time my clients are more afraid of me than the other way around," said Mistress Ava

Zhang. "That said, sex workers deal with a ninety-nine percent male clientele. That second half of the population is stronger than you and could kidnap you, and rape you, and kill you. I mean functionally, their bodies can do that. I'm not saying most men want to do that, but you have to always keep that in mind."

Professional dominatrixes also have to worry about the law. The Allow States and Victims to Fight Online Sex Trafficking Act (FOSTA)[7] and the Stop Enabling Sex Traffickers Act (SESTA)[8] were put into place in 2018 to fight sex trafficking. These laws have made it so websites such as Craigslist and Backpage (the latter was shuttered by the FBI in 2018) can be held liable if sex workers use them to post ads. There has been fierce opposition to these laws by free speech advocates and those who say that they actually endanger sex workers.[9] Opponents to the laws say that the laws prevent sex workers, who rely on the internet to help screen clients, avoid violence by sharing electronic "bad date" lists, and seek health care and other resources.[10]

Pro-dommes may be intuitive ninjas, but their intuition is no substitute for knowing that the law is on their side.

YOUR INTUITION AT WORK

In my own professional life, I often ignored my intuition out of fear that I was using my emotions to guide my thought process. What if I was wrong? I also didn't want to appear weak for relying on my feelings. I lacked the confidence in my own judgment to say, "I don't think this is a good idea."

It took years to be able to effectively use my intuition to buttress arguments in the workplace. I was way more persuasive if I said *why* I believed that a project was doomed to go south rather than just "knowing" that it would. Intuition told me that an initiative was likely to fail but digging into the data to show how similar projects tanked would prove my intuition to be correct.

It took practice for me to even trust my instincts in the first place. The first step was believing that my intuition was worth listening to. When I started to listen to my intuition, people started listening to *me*. I didn't want to be one of those people who said things like, "I had a feeling that wasn't going to work out, but I didn't want to be the one to say it."

I wanted to be the one to say it. I had to learn to say "this isn't a good idea and here's why."

Intuition isn't just for executive decision-making. It can also help us navigate the kind of awkward situations that arise in the workplace every day.

A female friend of mine, at a tech company, told me that she knew a male CEO was shady just by his physical presence. He hovered, he got too close, he drank too much.

"Even when he was wearing a suit, he gave off the vibe of having just stepped out of the shower," she said.

The problem was that she kept bumping into him at networking events. She didn't want to avoid attending industry meet-ups just because she had anxiety that he would be there. But her ick vibe was so strong, she asked her male business partner to rescue her if she was stuck alone in a room with him. So she wasn't at all shocked when, a few months later, he was forced to step down for sexual harassment and for creating an extremely hostile work environment for women.

It's also okay to use your intuition for your own gain. Here are some examples of using intuition to make power moves:

- Scheduling that talk for a raise in the morning after your boss has had his first cup of coffee rather than at the end of the day, when he's in a bad mood.

- Noticing that your manager has been coming to work in a suit and tie and leaving in the middle of the day for "appointments." Start updating your resume and talking points so that you're ready to throw your hat in the ring for his job when he gives his notice.

- Being aware that your boss may be struggling with family or child care issues and offering to take things off her plate so she can leave on time.

If you look around your office, see the free bagels are disappearing, empty desks, and angry emails from unpaid freelancers, you may intuit the good times are over—and it's time to start looking for a new job.

LESSON
#6

YOU MUST KEEP AN OPEN MIND

What's really cool about BDSM for women,
I think, is that it introduces a totally novel
concept into female sexuality: anarchy.

—GLORIA BRAME

We can't talk about kink without talking about the ele-
phant on the bookshelf.

If nothing else, E. L. James's *Fifty Shades of Grey* series
certainly had an impact on the way people talked about sex.
Since its publication in 2011, over 125 million mainstream
readers have been contemplating handcuffs, butt plugs, public
sex, humiliation, spanking, and mutual masturbation. In the
old days, if you didn't have a place where you could find and
peruse erotica, you had to know where to look for that kind of
thing. Your local lending library may not have had a naughty
books section but savvy readers have been sourcing scorching
sex scenes in Anne Rice novels for years.

For the very few of you who aren't familiar with what the
Fifty Shades saga is about, here's the Cliffs Notes: Shy, vir-
ginal college grad (Anastasia Steele) meets mysterious rich guy
(Christian Grey). He introduces her to BDSM. At first she's

shocked, but then, slowly but surely, she succumbs to his powerful, kinky spell and discovers her darkest inner desires. Endless orgasms ensue.

I knew the *Fifty Shades of Grey* books were a bona fide phenomenon when I saw them for sale at Costco. Suddenly, regular folks could read passages of the books to their partners and ask them, "What do you think of this?" And then say, "Um, I think it's pretty hot." It made kink into something . . . romantic. You could read the *Fifty Shades* books on the train or buy them at your local bookstore without feeling like a perv. Because how embarrassing could it be if all your friends (and their moms!) were reading about BDSM?

At La Domaine Esemar, the upscale BDSM château in the Berkshires where Mistress Couple worked as an innkeeper, fantasy exploration is an essential part of the experience. Guests come from all over the world to explore all their wildest fetish desires, including (but definitely not limited to) sensory deprivation, crossdressing, being hoisted aloft in a sex swing, and access to every sex toy under the sun, all under the guidance of the château's capable staff of dominants and submissives. One gentleman had a fantasy of being spit-roasted over a flame. The staff at La Domaine made it happen for the delighted (and afterward, only slightly singed) guest.

"The antidote to shame is bringing light to things and talking about them out in the open," Mistress Couple told me. "And I think that's why *Fifty Shades of Grey* was so popular. It's not because it was a good book, it's because people were finally talking about this thing publicly, and they could say, 'Oh, thank God. I can finally express that I'm into this and it's not going to be seen as sick or weird anymore.'"

But here's the thing about *Fifty Shades of Grey*. It's a kinky Cinderella story, but it's still a Cinderella story. Christian is a rich, handsome, dominant yet sensitive guy who knows what the timid Anastasia wants and needs and is able to "give" her endless orgasms. If Anastasia hadn't met him, who knows where she'd be? Maybe a successful editor in charge of her own destiny, but hey, that's not as sexy as a dude with a helicopter and a penchant for anal beads.

The kinky conversations that the books inspired were a breath of fresh air, but the underlying message was old as dirt. A dominant man and a submissive woman. A flawed but passionate knight in shining armor. A happily ever-after marriage with children.

"In real life, there's no guy on a horse to rescue you and solve your problems," said Hudsy Hawn. "Kink was just the third character in *Fifty Shades* that made it different than a Harlequin romance. The author just used kink to make it more interesting, but it still tapped into all of our silly little girl fantasies that the guy is going to swoop in and save us."

Still, the books got millions of women thinking differently about desire. It got men thinking too. While many pro-dommes cringe at the literary quality of the books, I spoke to many who credit E. L. James for getting more people interested in seeing and learning from a professional dominatrix. The books weren't just good for getting America's imaginations buzzing—they were good for business.

BORN KINKY OR OPEN TO KINK?

Many pro-dommes have told me that they were "born kinky," and always knew that the things they liked sexually were a little different from what others seemed to like. They liked to wrestle, pull hair, make their partners beg, pin down their arms; or they had dark fantasies about humiliation, objectification, role-play, and submission. It was those kind of things that sent a jolt of desire between their legs—playing with power, instead of romantic walks on the beach.

But not everyone is born with a whip in her hand and the knowledge that she was put on this earth to rule.

"I don't think anyone is born to dominate. I mean, no one feels particularly dominant when they're stopped by a police officer who pulls them over to give them a traffic ticket," said Janet W. Hardy, founder of Greenery Press and author, coauthor, and publisher of dozens of kink books, including *The Ethical Slut: A Practical Guide to Polyamory, Open Relationships, and Other Freedoms in Sex and Love* and *When Someone You Love Is Kinky*.

"I think that women who have been exposed at a younger age to the idea that women aren't supposed to be submissive are likelier to be comfortable with dominance," she said. "But I think all of us have to learn it. I believe we're an amazing mix of temperament and personality and learning and environment."

Sexual confidence isn't an inherited trait, like brown eyes or attached earlobes. Some of us don't figure it out until we're in our thirties, forties, fifties, or later.

Gloria Brame, the sex therapist and author, told me that she was definitely "born kinky."

"When I was young, the only time I was ever able to come during vanilla intercourse or when I masturbated was by heavily fantasizing about S&M," she said. "It wasn't until I was older that I had to accept that the only thing that really gave me ecstatic orgasms was the idea of something fucking kinky."

Taking our desire from fantasy to reality isn't always a smooth path.

"When I was twenty, I was dating this guy, he would do whatever I wanted him to do," Brame said. "It all came to a head one night when he asked me to live out a fantasy he'd read about in *Penthouse* magazine. It was for me to get dressed up in sexy heels and a garter belt and stockings. He handed me a leather belt and I whipped him a little and then he ran around the room like a dog on all fours and barking. I had no idea what he was doing, and I almost died of laughter.

"But as I whipped him, which at first I was just sort of pretending to do, I gave him a couple of good whacks and I didn't know where they came from," she said. "So I went to the bathroom and my panties were drenched. I was so ashamed. I just couldn't believe it, and I didn't want to do it again.

"I was the child of Holocaust survivors; I went to a socialist summer camp," said Brame. "I got very emotionally upset at the idea of violence, because I was a passive feminist hippie.

"A few years later, I was dating this incredible guy, I lusted after him like crazy, I couldn't get enough of him. I asked him to spank me and he started laughing and said, 'No, I only do the normal stuff.'

"It was awful because I thought I was in love with this guy. When he said that, it just really shut me right down on the kink front for a long time."

It's terrifying to get up the nerve to voice a fantasy and then not have it be received in the way you wish it had been.

"Rejection is super scary, and there's so much shame and stigma, especially around sexuality and BDSM," said Mistress Couple. "I think it makes it that much harder to talk about.

"I remember telling a boyfriend that I wanted him to spank me," said Couple. "I don't really remember how it came up but I just said it. I'm a pretty straightforward person in general, and he seemed kind of shocked. But then he was like, 'Oh, okay, I would be into that.' And when we went to do it, I think he thought that it was going to be a lightweight little kind of fantasy thing. And he was, like, golf clapping on my butt.

"And I was like, 'No, you can go harder.' I think that's what freaked him out. And he was like, 'I'm sorry, I just can't hit a woman.' And I really respected him in that moment, because I think that's a really good reason to struggle with doing BDSM with a partner. But I was like, 'You know what? I want you to hit me, and I'm giving you permission.'

"But he wasn't into it, he couldn't do it. So yeah, of course I was disappointed. But I continued to try to find a way to understand what I was looking for. And luckily, we had an open relationship, so he was okay with me exploring that."

While researching this book I spoke with professional dominatrixes with strict religious upbringings and those who grew up in traditional households. Many of them, despite having kinky leanings, suppressed them out of fear of being judged "abnormal" or feeling pressure to align their sexualities with what they saw in the movies. Salvation came to many of them in college, where they began to read books that piqued their interests and showed them that not only weren't they alone in the world but that there was an entire universe out there waiting for them.

"When I was twenty-nine, and I was ready for my truth to hit me," Brame said, "I awakened to myself as a kinky person. All of sudden it was like, bring it on. I want to be everywhere and experience everybody and see everything. And you know what? It gave me this whole new burst of enthusiasm for life and for men and for sex.

"And I never turned back."

MIXING PAIN AND PLEASURE

It's a myth that people who love kink get off on being hurt or by hurting others. In fact, many pro-dommes describe their work as healing. It's about being receptive to someone else's desires and responding with care for the other's well-being. It's always more about the heart than the hurt. People seek out professional dominatrixes because they want to be heard and seen as human beings who may have inclinations and desires that are different from the norm.

"My purpose is to bring joy to people in really unconventional ways, to connect people to themselves and to me," said Mistress Ava Zhang. "One of the first things that the mainstream sees in how BDSM is presented is it's just somebody inflicting pain on another person. But really, to submit is to essentially tell the other person, 'I want to be vulnerable to you. I want to be naked in front of you. I want to shed my pretenses. I want you to see me.'"

At first, I didn't understand how pain could be sexually pleasurable at all. I'd only been hit a few times in my life, and I definitely didn't enjoy it. One time, while playing soccer, two girls clotheslined me, and I had to limp off the field with scraped knees and a bloody nose. When I was in elementary school, my best friend punched me in the stomach. (She has since apologized.) One time, while playing doubles tennis, I was hit so hard in the face with a racquet that I woke up on the court seeing little cartoon birds.

Sexually, I associated pain with alarm bells, and the need to stop everything immediately. At the same time, I'd been lucky to have had partners who were adventurous and down to try new things. I knew that a well-timed consensual slap on the ass from a lover could cause my bells to ring in an entirely different way.

If kink was about being open-minded, I wanted to know what it was like to be "hurt" by a professional. So I made an appointment with my professional dominatrix friend Lola and asked her if she'd mind taking me through the steps of negotiating a scene and then seeing it through with me.

Lola enthusiastically agreed on the condition that I send her a detailed email of what I'd like to do and experience.

I told my husband about my plan and, once he felt convinced that I was meeting with a thoughtful and trustworthy person, he told me not to hold back. But still, it was a lot to mull over. I wasn't sure what I wanted to do or experience. I knew that Lola prided herself on her impact skills. While researching the book, she and I attended events together and I'd watched in awe as she wielded floggers and paddles with sadistic precision, like an artist spattering paint across a canvas.

A few days later, I emailed her back and requested mild to moderate impact, teasing, exhibition (standing in front of her, naked or in underwear), and light bondage. I also gave her permission to say humiliating things to me ("look at you, you nasty girl," but not "you disgusting pig").

"You can hurt me," I wrote. "But don't hurt my feelings."

She wrote back enthusiastically and asked more questions to clarify a few things. Did I want role-play? How did I feel about blindfolds? What about a gag? I told her I was more interested in sensation play than role-play and that all the other stuff would be cool as long as she kept in mind that I was a total beginner and had never experienced anything like this before. We negotiated every aspect of our meet-up so that nothing would be left to chance.

A few days later, I arrived at her apartment in Brooklyn with a store-bought chocolate babka (I'm a nice person; I never go to someone's house empty-handed). She welcomed me with a big hug and offered me a glass of water. We both knew that it wouldn't be like a regular client session, since we were friends, but she said she'd do her best to replicate one the best she could. I told her that I was in her hands and to go for it. We confirmed safe words, and we were off to the races.

Since it was my fantasy, I wore lingerie under my dress.

When she saw my black lace Savage X Fenty scanties, she decided to get into the spirit and changed into a black bustier and high heels. The session felt more like a slumber party than a sin-fest. She told me to kneel in front of her and she held my head to her stomach in order to signal that the scene was beginning and to create a feeling of bonding between us. I closed my eyes and I began trembling as I heard her reach for all the tools she'd set out for me.

Friends, I cannot remember everything that happened in the next hour, because it was all a sweet and shocking blur, but here's what I can recall. She had me kneel on her beautiful peach-rose-colored couch, and then ran the falls of a suede flogger between my shoulder blades, making me shiver. She began hitting me with it lightly, across my back. Then she started to go a little harder and I began to sweat. Later I would describe the lashings like a ribbon, very soft but with a knife-like edge. There was a sting and then . . . a rush of pleasure. It was daylight outside; the sun shone through her curtains. Cars were honking; people were outside shopping, carrying groceries, riding their bikes. And yet here I was, doing this outrageous and sensual thing, my hands against the wall as the flogger began to crack louder against my skin. At one point, she snapped the flogger right between my shoulder blades. The explosion of sound made me gasp. "That was too hard, wasn't it?" she asked, rubbing my back. "No," I breathed, surprised. "It wasn't."

She tied my wrists together using a rose-colored rope that matched her sofa, pulled it between my legs, and carefully tied my ankles together. She used paddles and her bare hands to spank me. Then she had me stand in front of her and take off all my clothes. She circled me, while I stood there, breathless and blushing. Finally, she had me kneel in front of her again and thank her. "Thank you, Mistress," I said.

When I sat up, she was sitting on the couch, smiling. "So," she said. "What did you think?"

I blinked a few times. My whole body was tingling and my face was flushed. I felt like I'd just finished a really intense workout. Everything felt upside down and turned around. "That was amazing," I said. "I want to do that again!"

We hugged goodbye and I got into a cab and headed home, my mind swimming. I'd never experienced anything so sexual without worrying about another person's arousal, and having to manage it in return.

Because honestly, aside from paying for a massage at a spa, when do we as women ever get the chance to just enjoy a sensual experience without feeling pressure to reciprocate? The best part of getting a professional massage is not having to jump off the table and say, "Now your turn!" In and out of bed, I'd always felt pressure to make sure everyone was having fun, even at the sake of my own enjoyment. To experience something that was just for my pleasure was . . . mind-blowing.

It was a life-changing experience and I have not been the same since, and I hope I never will be again.

BE OPEN TO FANTASIES

There's a misconception that if you have a dark fantasy it means there's something hidden in you, and if you indulge it, it's going to come out in unexpected ways and make you a cruel person.

"It's just not true, and in fact, the message that you shouldn't think about those things, that you shouldn't act on them, actually makes people repress things and then they come out years later in weird, unrecognizable ways," said Tina Horn. "Then it's less recognizable and actually dark. And much harder to deal with."

Our fantasies can scare us. What does it say about you as a feminist if you secretly dream of being tied up, spanked, gawked at, or serving as the main attraction in a gang bang? What does it say about you as a person if you dream of hurting someone else? Could you be a good mother if you think about having sordid threesomes with strangers? The internet is a buffet of pornographic images, videos, and erotica tailored to every kink under the sun. Who among us hasn't seen or read something that both horrified and aroused?

When I was a teenager, I had a lot of dirty thoughts. Some were typical teenage stuff—making out with a boyfriend in a huge bed in an empty house or passionate sex with a mystery guy (even though I hadn't had sex yet). But I also had ones that worried me. I imagined lying on a bench in a gym locker room while an older woman seduced me, but I was powerless to stop her. In another fantasy I was being forced to pledge a sorority, and the other girls teased me mercilessly and ordered me to give them orgasms by any means necessary. I imagined being held down and forced to do terrible things by faceless boys and faceless teachers. What did it all mean? In real life, I was afraid of the gym, of mean girls, and of being put in a forced or violent situation with men. In real life, I guarded my virginity. But in my fantasies, things went to places that didn't make sense.

Now that I'm older, I know that all teenagers and young adults have crazy fantasies—and that they don't end with adulthood. Playing with kink gives us permission to keep using our imagination and keep digging into our sexual subconscious. It keeps us open-minded so we don't get too comfortable with one definition of what sex is supposed to be.

My theory? I think most of us are born a little kinky, but not many of us keep that wild part of ourselves alive over the years. Remember how wild you were in your early twenties? For a lot of us it was a freer time; we had fewer responsibilities and needed fewer things to make us happy. Experimenting with sex with fun, willing partners didn't cost a thing; all we needed was a bed, some music, and a door that closed.

But then something happens. We stop exploring. Our thoughts and fantasies don't go away, but our willingness to explore them fizzles out. Maybe we got married and had kids. Maybe life threw us curveballs that set us back, and put realizing sexual fantasies on the back burner. We can't just snap our fingers and bring back our younger selves, so full of come-hither desire. That said, it's never too late to dig into our fantasy archive and open ourselves up to new experiences, baby steps at a time.

"I encourage people to go exploring for images from a movie or passages from erotica," said Mistress Couple. "Something that made you clench your legs together a little bit."

Justin Lehmiller, PhD, a fellow of the Kinsey Institute and the author of *Tell Me What You Want: The Science of Sexual Desire and How It Can Help You Improve Your Sex Life*, surveyed more than four thousand Americans to find out what turned them on. So what gets America hot and bothered? Per his study, the three top fantasies for both men and women include sex with multiple partners, rough sex, and wild positions that test the laws of the Bible and, in some cases, time and space.

The results of Lehmiller's survey of everyday Americans were rife with kink. Sixty percent of survey participants reported fantasies about inflicting physical pain on someone else during sex. Sixty-five percent said they fantasized about receiving physical pain during sex. Other NSFW fantasies included group sex, whippings, spankings, forced domination, watching or being "forced to watch," and humiliation of all kinds. His findings went against the societal belief that in bed, all men love to dominate and women are naturally submissive. Women were more likely than men to have fantasized about both giving and receiving pain.

We may not be born with our kinks, but our early sexual experiences can definitely inform our wild fantasies. Lehmiller found that an unusual (but positive) first sexual experience was linked to fantasies about BDSM, taboo sex acts, gender bending, and emotionless sex. Just as our taboo fantasies evolve, many stem from actual childhood experiences. The things we experience in our youth can put a stamp on us, shaping our kinks and fetishes for our entire adult lives. While he observed a connection between respondents who reported having been the victim of a sex crime with BDSM fantasies, he was careful not to overstate the link. Those who had *not* been the victim of sexual violence reported more kinky longings than those who did. We all process our past sexual joys and traumas differently. But our sexual fantasies, even the darkest ones, can actually help us heal and grow. They can help us understand ourselves better. We can be our truest selves in our deepest thoughts.

"You're playing make-believe. Why? Because it's satisfying," said Tina Horn. "Why? Because we want the things that we don't have."

And yet less than a third of participants reported having acted out their biggest sexual fantasy. It makes sense. Organizing a threesome is hard enough, finding a roadhouse full of drunk cowboys to ravage you in a debauched yet consensual manner would be a heroic logistical feat. It can be hard to find a partner who can see a fantasy through with you to its completion. It can be hard to put a dream into words. That said, we can tear off pieces of our fantasies. We can start small.

"I think every woman needs to remember that there are no 'shoulds.' That's what's really cool about BDSM for women—it introduces a totally novel concept into female sexuality," said Gloria Brame. "Which is anarchy." We can make it happen for ourselves. We can be our own Christine Greys.

THE POWER OF THE

BODY

YOUR BODY
DESERVES WORSHIP

Who told you that the shame was yours to carry?

—DAWN SERRA

I blame Michelle Pfeiffer for making me want to quit women's magazines.

True story. When I was twenty-two, I got my first job at a big women's magazine. I was a fact checker. It was my job to read articles in the magazine and make sure that the names of people and products were spelled correctly, that the ages of celebrities matched the age their PR person insisted they were, and that the carefully edited quotes from recorded interviews were close enough to the transcript that they would hold up under scrutiny.

I'd always wanted to work at a magazine, mostly because I'd been so deeply touched and transformed by *Sassy* magazine in my teens. *Sassy*, which lasted only four years in print, was unique in its inclusion of models of color, frank discussions of sexual and mental health, and recommendations of books, music, and films by female artists. My early days in women's magazines proved to be a lot less inspiring. For every story about a "real woman" who overcame adversity, there were dozens more that promoted dopey fashion (low-rise jeans! thongs!), ill-advised beauty tips (self-tanner for everyone!), and baffling sex trends (do you remember "vajazzle-ing"? I hope history doesn't).

Anyway, back to Michelle Pfeiffer. One day, I wandered past the art department and saw that the editors were choosing between two glossy photos for the cover. In one photo, Pfeiffer wore a red dress, in the other, she wore a blue dress. In both, she was smiling, her hand on her hip, and chic, her head held tight. She was forty-four and looked gorgeous, effervescent.

But when I looked closer I saw that someone had circled all the parts of her face and body that would need to be "corrected" with Photoshop. Comments included: "man hands," "bony collarbone," "nip in waist," "trim jawline," "armpit wrinkles" (!). Other problem areas: breast volume, bony elbows, crow's-feet. For the final cover, they not only "fixed" her imperfections, they swapped the head of the red dress Michelle and transplanted it on the blue dress Michelle.

In the early 2000s, before readers became aware of how Photoshopped celebrity photos really were, this was standard operating procedure. I saw Faith Hill's arm fat trimmed to the point where she looked like Gumby. Jennifer Aniston's body parts were chopped, blurred, and pasted until she resembled a creepy cardboard cutout. I can never forget how poor Julia Roberts looked after having received a total head to body transplant for an ill-conceived magazine cover. My colleagues and I dubbed her "Franken-Julia."

But Jesus fucking Christ, I wondered. If Michelle Pfeiffer, Julia Roberts, and Faith Hill didn't hold up to the standard of beauty to sell a magazine, what hope did I have? I was comparing myself to a fantasy that the stars themselves couldn't live up to.

"GODDESS" VS. GODDESS

Gaze upon the dominatrix, if you dare.

Start at her feet, which are soft and arched, each toe painted a fiery red, a sinister purple, or a deceptively sweet pink. To touch them is an honor; to kiss them, a sacred privilege. She towers over you in high heels or shiny leather boots with heels that narrow to knife points. If she allows you to lick the soles, you'll weep with gratitude. If she rests her heel against your face and presses the spike into your temple, her laughter will drown out your whimpers.

Behold her ankles that curve upward into strong, muscular calves and thighs that can crush a man's ribs or bend him to her will. She has an Amazon's stance, her latex or stocking-clad leg poised to send CEOs and executives reeling. Many have cowered at these legs, their eyes shining with fear and desire. If she's feeling generous, she may allow a glimpse of bare thigh under her skirt, where her garter belt meets the top of her stockings. Or, if it's the luckiest day of your life, a brush of this flesh against your arm. But don't think you've seen or felt anything she didn't mean for you to see or feel. Everything is calculated. She'll show you just enough to make you believe that you may one day know that beacon of light between her legs. Ha, keep dreaming.

Her hips are heaven, flaring out from her waist, nipped in by a corset. Her curves are ocean swells, rising, falling, punishing, awe-inspiring. Her back is straight and strong. Her breasts are hidden behind glossy armor. When she presses your face into them, you will be lost. Men have cried there, their bodies red and raw from having been beaten by strong arms with tools of destruction wielded by sure hands. Her fingernails are filed to rounded points. She will rake your back with them and then soothe your wounds with gentle mercy.

Looking into her face, if she lets you, is like gazing into the sun. Her curling red lips reveal her teeth when she smiles or sneers. Her eyes glitter as you writhe in aroused agony. The more you suffer, the more she delights. She paints her face with black ink and scarlet lipstick, or perhaps she wears no makeup at all. It doesn't matter. She is utterly at home in her skin; any cosmetics she applies are for her own edification and pleasure. Her tattoos are her own symbols; they mark her experience, her triumphs, her lessons, her tragedies. Her body is utterly hers to control and display. Her laughter is the ringing bell that seals your fate.

You are a toy, a speck, a slave to her desire. Her body is the temple, and you are helpless before her altar.

Here's the thing. It's a fantasy. Men, mostly wealthy and white, pay a lot of money to submit to a certain type of woman who aligns with their fantasies. While some seek out a professional dominatrix based on her intelligence and her dedication to her craft and ethos, there are just as many men who "domme-shop," making the rounds to different pro-dommes in a city to see what they look like in person, test out their skills, and then move on to the next one.

Despite what we see in the mainstream media, pro-dommes are not tall, slender ice queens or soulless fembots in latex. They look like us. They're muscular, they're petite, they've got natural hair, they're androgynous, they're voluptuous, they've got braids, they've got bellies, they've got tattoos. They've got goth style, they're prim and proper, they've got legs for days, their skin is pale as milk, they're all shades of brown. They're six foot two, they're four foot ten. They're an AA cup, they're a EEE cup. They've got dimples, piercings, and cellulite. They've got big, gorgeous asses, they've got high arches and perfect toes, they've got freckles and moles and scars and laugh lines.

The difference between pro-dommes and the rest of us is that they work especially hard to find ways to love themselves and to understand the roles their faces and bodies play at work and when they're alone at night, brushing their teeth. During the day, they may feel the thrill of having a client quiver at their feet, breathlessly whispering their name, but when the latex is off, they have a lot of the same body issues as the rest of us.

You may not have a rich white man on his knees in front of you, handing you cash for the mere privilege of breathing your air, but it never hurts to start thinking about your body for its strengths rather than its weaknesses, and to stop obsessing all about your many flaws.

After all, who told you they were flaws in the first place?

"We need not do anything other than turn on a television for evidence affirming how desperately our society, our world, needs an extreme force of self-love to counter the constant barrage of shame, discrimination, and body-based oppression enacted against us daily," writes Sonya Renee Taylor in *The Body Is Not an Apology: The Power of Radical Self Love*.[1] "Television shows like *The Biggest Loser* encourage dangerous and unsustainable exercise and food restriction for their contestants while using their bodies as fodder for our entertainment and reinforcing the notion that the most undesirable body one can have is a fat body."

True story: I was once in a bar with some acquaintances and this one guy staggered over to me, drunk, red-faced, and sweaty. He nudged me and motioned to a cute girl laughing with her friends and said, "Well, it's three a.m. Time to take it up a weight class."

Charming.

Dawn Serra is a sex and relationship coach (but not a professional dominatrix) who works with individuals and couples who want to figure out what's holding them back from enjoying sex, communicating desire effectively, and managing the complex emotions that come with intimacy. In her work, she emphasizes the relationship between body shame and sexual inhibitions.

"Maybe you were shamed by your parents about your body or the food you ate. Maybe you were caught masturbating and told you were sinful or disgusting," she said.[2] "Ask yourself this: Who told you that the shame was yours to carry? Do you believe them? Have you actually seen evidence to prove that what they said to you is true?"

The families that raised us, the magazines we read, the images we grew up with—they weren't the reliable narrators we thought they were.

"After we ask these questions of ourselves, we can start to find ways to set that shame down, because it belonged to our mothers or fathers, or it belonged to a community that we're no longer a part of, to friends that we don't even associate with anymore. Then it's not yours to carry around anymore," Serra said.

"Then you can start to see yourself for who you really are."

OUR BODIES DESERVE SPACE

In the dungeon, men must ask a pro-domme's permission to touch an article of her clothing or a part of her body. Unwanted touching in-session will result in an immediate end—to the scene and, if necessary, the relationship.

If only our space was as respected outside of the dungeon. When we talk about space, we're not only talking about getting manspreading dudes to shove over so we can sit comfortably on trains and planes. I'm talking about how owning our physical bodies affects our access to power.

Are you a trans person? Your right to use a bathroom is still up for grabs depending on the state you live in, and even if you're allowed to go in, your safety isn't guaranteed. Having a trans body, no matter what you wear, is dangerous. A National Transgender Discrimination Survey found that 40 percent of participants who presented ID that didn't match their gender presentation were harassed, 15 percent were asked to leave an establishment, and 3 percent were assaulted.[3]

Women of the world, we can't even pee, shit, or menstruate in peace.

Public bathrooms don't have working tampon machines (and if they do, who knows how long those dusty things have been jammed in there). Working women have to pump their breast milk in dirty bathrooms or supply closets. A few states have eliminated the "period tax" (a tax on menstrual products), but most American women are still paying out of pocket to not free-bleed. In 2018, Representative Sean Maloney (D-NY) went public about how ludicrous it was that his office wasn't allowed to expense thirty-seven dollars to pay for sanitary supplies for visitors and female staff. Critics howled and dubbed it "Tampongate."[4]

According to a 2019 report from WaterAid, 335 million girls go to school without water and soap available for washing their hands when changing sanitary pads. Girls in sub-Saharan Africa, Asia, and South America report feeling fear, shame, and embarrassment due to the lack of information, support, and facilities to manage their menstruation in school.[5]

Our bodies are at once too tempting to be near, and not valued enough to be taken seriously.

The #MeToo movement may have brought sexual harassment, unwanted touching, rape, assault, and domestic violence out of the shadows, but it's also yielding new and shitty consequences. Male managers report wanting to distance themselves from women in the workplace out of fear of being accused of inappropriate conduct.[6] *Bloomberg* writers Gillian Tan and Katia Porzecanski dubbed this the "Pence Effect"[7] after Vice President Mike Pence, who famously said he avoids dining alone with any woman other than his wife.[8]

"In finance," Tan and Porzecanski write, "the overarching impact can be, in essence, gender segregation."

Criado Perez, in *Invisible Women*, writes that, for women around the world, the simple act of getting to and from work is a minefield of harassment, unwanted touching, and "a feeling of sexual menace." Women constantly have look over their shoulder to make sure they're not being followed, comply with requests to "smile," or fear the repercussions if they don't.[9]

In the world of BDSM, people get called out for nonconsensual touching. Many kinky events have zero-tolerance policies; those who don't abide are asked to leave and not come back. But outside in the vanilla world, professional dominatrixes battle for their personal space like the rest of us.

"A man's belief that he's entitled to our attention and bodies is astounding," said Dia Domina Dynasty. "I'm acutely aware of how, in public spaces such as streets and mass transportation, even social media where people are sharing spaces, men tend to violate women's spaces with no awareness of what they're doing.

"I can't go around just telling everybody, 'Don't touch me,' but I can convey it energetically," said Dynasty. "I wear a lot of black, I walk rapidly, and I do not display any sense of confusion."

YOUR FACE FOR THE WORLD TO JUDGE

I am a beauty fanatic and my face is a canvas for self-expression. Some of my most cherished memories are of watching my mother and my grandmother sit in front of their makeup mirrors, playing with their powders and pencils, the electric blues, dusty roses, deep caramels, and tiny black mascara brushes. How exhilarating to put on a new face one day and then another the next! Makeup can allow us to be our other selves, the ones we're afraid to be after we wash our faces at night. Red lipstick can make us feel invincible. Black lipstick shows the world that we are not to be messed with. Green lipstick can make us feel more beautiful than a pink lipstick ever could.

"There's joy to be had in nourishing your looks in a way that sort of forces you to appreciate them. I really think that if I had less of a face routine, I wouldn't feel as positively about aging," writes Autumn Whitefield-Madrano in her book *Face Value: The Hidden Way Beauty Shapes Women's Lives.*[10] "I'm not troubled by the fine lines I'm seeing develop; I'm acknowledging them and welcoming them as a part of who I am today."

Things have changed at the beauty counter. There's never been a wider selection of makeup shades to suit so many skin shades. Women have spoken, and any skin care or cosmetics company that doesn't offer a wide selection of foundation, concealer, or powder shades is now hopelessly behind the times, missing out on a huge audience of women with plenty of money to spend. In beauty and skin care campaigns we see head scarves, round cheeks, single lids, big noses, gapped teeth, and freckly foreheads. There's gray hair, faces with (the right amount of) wrinkles. This is a good thing! But we can also afford to think critically about what's being sold to us at the makeup counter.

There's nothing wrong with contouring sticks and high-lighters, as long as we're aware of the parts of our faces our culture is telling us to shade, conceal, or show off. Who is telling us that our noses need narrowing, our jawlines need contouring, our cheekbones highlighting? Why are some lip shades "kissable"? Is the color "orgasm" the color of every woman's face when she has an orgasm? (I'm more of a blotchy rose.)

We're hammered with so many confusing and contradictory messages about how our bodies should look. Be yourself! Be healthy! Lose the weight! You're perfect the way you are! Strong is the new skinny! Wait, should I love the skin I'm in? Or should I buy a waist trainer so I can . . . embrace my curves? The concept of body positivity went from a fat-acceptance movement aimed at fighting against medical and societal discrimination against overweight people, to beauty and fashion marketing babble, a craven attempt to corner new demographics and increase profits.

"Media in our culture is often aimed at women in a way that creates self-doubt and a feeling of inadequacy," said Dia Domina Dynasty. "It's nearly impossible to feel good after browsing through social media or any 'fashion' magazine because of so many unrealistic body types being displayed as the 'norm.' So instead, we find ourselves 'lacking' a certain purse or suddenly feeling that our belly is too round or our lips aren't plump enough."

The language of body positivity has been watered down, Instagrammed, monetized, and sold to us at a premium. "Femvertising," a term for using feminism and images of powerful women to sell products, is nothing new. In 1968, Phillip Morris told women that they'd come a long way, baby—so didn't they deserve to smoke a slender, ladylike Virginia Slim? In 2019, I can feel awesome buying a "Girl Power" shade of pink blush and then I can eat cereal that will help me think about "what I'll gain when I lose." Why do we fall for it? We want to buy products that align with our views of how we wish the world could be. We want to feel like our purchases are serving us, and not the other way around.

Why do women with PhDs plunk down sixty dollars for "elixirs" and "anti-aging serums," when we know full well that there are no witches working at big cosmetic companies (and if there are, please email me, I have many questions)? Maybe because they're afraid not to. I've felt pressure to get Botox out of fears that my ideas will be tossed aside and disregarded if I don't appear younger than I am. But Botox is expensive! Is it an investment in my career or a quarterly investment in self-doubt? What kind of force can I be if I'm unsure of the face I'm putting out in the world?

There have been cases of skin-lightening creams and Brazilian hair straighteners, products that are peddled to women all over the world to achieve a more Western look, shown to contain high levels of toxic chemicals. According to the *American Journal of Obstetrics and Gynecology*, "racial discrimination based on European beauty norms can lead to internalized racism, body shame, and skin tone dissatisfaction, factors that can influence product use to achieve straighter hair or lighter skin."[10]

A moisturizer is just a moisturizer, until it's actually about ageism. A concealer is just a concealer, until it's really about covering up the scars underneath. A bronzer is just a bronzer until you find white female beauty vloggers using it to emulate the appearances of women of color. Then it's about racism. In short, a lip liner is just a lip liner—until it's political.

■ ■ ■

Back when I was working in women's magazines, I saw a teenaged Slovenian model waiting patiently on a chair in the glass enclosed lobby, holding her enormous portfolio in her lap. She was crying.

"I have to go to the bathroom, but I'm waiting for someone to come get me," she told me.

I felt so terrible for her. She was just a kid, lost in a big city, being treated like a commodity for her looks, struggling with her English, and was too scared and intimidated to ask a stranger for help. After I showed her where the restroom was, she told me that she was living in an apartment with seven other girls and that she'd been out all day meeting with different magazines. Her feet hurt.

How powerful was her youth and beauty when someone was holding her visa and she was too afraid to ask where the bathroom is?

Beyond the makeup counter, we're paying to exist as women.

Consider the "pink tax," the subtle difference in price for the same product when one version is aimed specifically at women. "Manufacturers can find some consumers who are not aware of price differences, or are willing to pay for something that's really the same as the male version," Ian Parkman, assistant professor of marketing at the University of Portland, told *U.S. News & World Report* in 2016. "[With razors], the blue version [might be] $1.99, and the pink razor [might be] $2.50, but pink plastic versus blue plastic can't explain the price difference."[11]

Heading to the drugstore to pick up a few things, but want to stay on budget? Be sure to bring your calculator and reading glasses so you can do some fun math regarding price per ounce and to make sure the "pink" laxatives have the same amount of active ingredient as the nonpink laxatives. Men with erectile dysfunction can fill their Cialis or Viagra prescriptions anywhere, but our health insurers and employers can dictate what birth control is covered. But what if you're a virtuous married woman who wants a family but also suffers from endometriosis? If you've got a religious employer, have fun paying for it out of pocket.[12]

Our shirts cost more to dry-clean,[13] our jeans cost more, and toys aimed at girls cost more than toys aimed at boys.[14] It starts at the cradle. Onesies for baby girls cost more than onesies for baby boys.[15] In the age of gender-reveal parties and hand-wringing over our sexualities and identities, we can't even buy our daughters a yellow shirt without making a political statement.

Earlier, I talked about the joy of makeup and beauty, but for most professional women, coming into work without makeup isn't an option—unless you want to risk a scolding from your boss for "unprofessional appearance." Your parking may be validated, but you will need to pay more than men for your haircuts and shoes. If you work in an executive role, you will be paying for blow-outs, manicures, hosiery, dry cleaning, late-night cab rides home, and, if you're in a competitive industry where ageism is rampant, Botox and plastic surgery.

So what can you do about it? You can vote with your wallet and call bullshit on gendered clothing for kids, buy men's products with similar ingredients to those in women's products, and buy a men's medium instead of a women's large. You can donate to organizations that provide sanitary supplies to girls in need. You can be skeptical of all the pink ribbon products jammed down your throat during Breast Cancer Awareness Month and look at the fine print to make sure that the money actually goes toward organizations that actually do something to fund a cure.

You can demand that your purchases serve you.

Maybe I'm just cynical, but when I read about bodies as being "celebrated" instead of accepted, I feel like I'm being talked down to.

Once upon a time, I thought that famous Dove Campaign for Real Beauty with all the different sizes and shapes of women was pretty awesome. As I walked through the subway station, it was nice to see women in ads with bodies that looked like mine, soft shoulders, big thighs, et cetera. It was a nice break for the eye. I'd become so skeptical, so I was trying hard not to be a hater. A lot of women said they loved the ads; they felt seen.

In 2013, I found myself in a large auditorium in midtown Manhattan, attending a presentation by Dove's marketing team, and watched as executives introduced the long-form video ad "Dove Real Beauty Sketches."

Dubbed (by Dove) as a "daring beauty experiment," the video showed women describing their own physical appearances to a police sketch artist. Then a stranger describes the same woman to the artist. And when the woman sees the two sketches and the difference between how she sees herself and how others see her, it's Niagara Falls. I didn't feel empowered watching "real women" cry upon realizing how cruel they'd been to themselves. I felt manipulated. Why did it take so many tears to sell women soap and deodorant?

In her book, Whitefield-Madrano talks a lot about the Dove Campaign for Real Beauty and all the ways it was lauded for its concept of encouraging women to feel better about themselves. But in retrospect, she suggests, it was as manipulative as any other beauty ad campaign.

"Companies get to appear to be standing alongside their critics while continuing to ultimately reinforce the narrative that garnered the criticism in the first place," she wrote.

When Whitefield-Madrano spoke to her friend Mary about Dove's ad strategy, she put it bluntly. "It's like Dove expected fat women to be grateful to them for acknowledging that we exist."

Therein lies the problem. We're waiting for brands to recognize our bodies as beautiful when it's always been up to us to do it for ourselves.

One spring afternoon, I attended a "female supremacy" meeting in a midtown dungeon. Men were allowed to attend the event, provided they paid $20 to be there and sat on the floor. The women, most of them pro-dommes, sat on comfy couches, drank tea, and talked about current events and all the things that made them angry. The conversation turned to money and the disparate cost of living between men and women.

I asked one of the pro-dommes about her practice of asking her clients to pay additional financial "tributes" in addition to her BDSM services. Her response? "Because we spend a fortune to live up to the standards of beauty that society has declared we must abide by. It affects how much we make, and how well we're treated. They reap the benefits of our efforts, and therefore they should pay."

Mic drop. Because, damn, we pay a lot to fit in, to be accepted, to turn our lovers on, to stay in shape, to be loved, and to stay relevant in our respective careers. My husband and I split the costs of our mortgage, our pet care, our health insurance, but I never thought of asking him to split the cost of my birth control, or my Weight Watchers subscription, or the astronomical cost of bleaching my hair blonde. We both know that it costs more to be me than it costs to be him. In fact, he'd probably be happy to chip in. I just never thought of asking him to do it.

Your body deserves worship, but most of us pay a lot of money to feel worthy of that worship. Shit, we pay a lot of money just to feel worthy of existing.

So the next time your partner comments that he'd go down on you more if you had less pubic hair, tell him to fork over seventy-five dollars and the cost of exfoliating cream to prevent ingrown hairs or shut the fuck up about it. You can trim it, bleach it, grow it, and show it. It's your goddamned pubic hair.

"Consider going on a media diet or simply become aware that there are so many psychic assaults on our self-esteem just to get us to buy more things," said Dynasty.

"Advertising will sneak itself into so many spaces that slip below our consciousness, so this is a conscientious practice. It's taken me a very long time and I still slip sometimes."

Because if your pain is actually society's gain, then it's time to think about who's being worshipped and who's being screwed.

LESSON #8

YOUR CLOTHING
GIVES YOU POWER

If you're dressed in head-to-toe latex or leather,
people are gonna make some assumptions about you.
Probably that you're interesting, at the very least.

—THE BARONESS

Quick exercise. Close your eyes and imagine walking into a conference room, slamming down your bag, looking a bunch of scared coworkers in the eyes, and saying, "Listen up, assholes. Things are about to change around here."

What are you wearing?

Not sure? Here's what I'm wearing in my "I own 51 percent of this company" fantasy:

A black silk blazer nipped at the waist, matching pencil skirt. White shirt, cuffs, collar opened one button. My dark hair is parted on the side and wavy, like Lauren Bacall in the 1946 film noir *The Big Sleep*. Under my clothes, where no one can see, I'm wearing expensive French lingerie. My thigh-high stockings hooked to my garter belt make me feel like I've got gun holsters on my thighs. My lips are red and my jewelry is heavy and gold. I'm wearing "don't fuck with me, fellas" heels.

After I finish telling a boardroom full of scared men in cheap, sweaty suits to stop giving me excuses and start coming up with some goddamned solutions, I stroll into my corner office and close the door. Then, I dial my loyal male assistant on speakerphone and tell him to cancel my lunch with so-and-so. Then I light a cigarette, spin my rich burgundy leather chair around, and contemplate the glittering city skyline. It's all mine.

In my fantasy, my clothes tell the world that I'm a woman with big-dick energy. My desk is bigger than your desk. My paycheck is bigger than your paycheck. I do not suffer fools. I'm tough but fair. I know what I want and I do not settle for second best. My employees are loyal to me because I value what they do and I pay them well. I can smell bullshit a mile away. I am a fucking queen.

Let's keep going, because frankly, I'm enjoying this.

When I come home at night, I take off my clothes and put on a pale gray, 1000-thread-count, ankle-length cotton robe and walk into my bathroom, my place of solitude, replete with Moroccan tile and a skylight that allows me to see the moon and stars. I sink into a deliciously warm bubble bath. I'm enveloped in the scent of Miami Beach: gardenias, ocean salt, and coconut. Once I'm done soaking, exfoliating, shaving, and dreaming, I towel off, and then head back into my bedroom. I put on a silk nightgown and slide under soft sheets custommade for me in a purple so dark it almost appears black. I stretch out, pick a novel off my nightstand, and curl up. Finally, drowsy and peaceful, I drift off to sleep. My king-sized bed feels like a raft floating on a calm sea.

In my fantasy, it's just me, my luxury, and the knowledge that I can have the affections of a man if I want them and, of course, that there's money in the bank.

Fin.

Okay, do I really want fabulous clothing, luscious bedding, a corner office, and a bathroom with a tub the size of an Olympic-sized swimming pool? Hell yeah. But back to clothing. What I wear in my fantasy harnesses a feeling, an attitude: a desire for power, independence, and extreme confidence. It projects everything about myself that I want the world to see.

I didn't want to dress for someone else's success. I wanted a style that I could call my own. But that would require more than a new wardrobe. It would require an entirely new mind-set.

■ ■ ■

The Baroness[1] is a legendary designer of latex clothing with a small shop in New York City's East Village. When Lady Gaga wanted something eye-popping to wear in her video for her song "Born This Way," The Baroness designed an amber latex collar that made her look like an alien empress. When Beyoncé hit the carpet at the 2016 Met Ball in a glossy rosy-peach latex Givenchy gown, it was The Baroness who oversaw every aspect of its fit. She has created bold and expressive costumes for the FX series *Pose* to showcase the wildly creative ballroom dance culture of the late 1980s and early 1990s. Fashion-forward artists like Solange Knowles, Nicki Minaj, Sia, and Katy Perry have worn her creations. Her work has been photographed for *Vogue Italia*, *Interview*, and countless magazines that worship the art of couture fetish fashion.

Latex is tight; it has a unique scent. You literally need to lubricate your body to put it on (I found this out firsthand). It makes sounds when you snap it. It hugs you; you feel it against every inch of your body. Latex is the material of desire. It's unapologetically kinky. It's shiny and clingy; it's the stuff of superheroes.

The Baroness's outrageous costumes are the stuff of New

York City kink party legend. Do you want to dress like a nun, a cruel governess, a nurse, a Disney character, or a warrior princess? She will design your dream in latex. A male customer may feel empowered to express a darker, kinkier, secret part of himself that he's never shared with anyone before. A nonbinary person may see their body as it looks in their dreams. The Baroness dresses everyone with love, but also with a critical eye.

The Baroness creates kink couture that goes way beyond basic black. In her cheerful shop, you can buy red opera-length fingerless latex gloves, electric blue latex miniskirts, and elegant dresses in pearly silver. She takes her inspiration from the golden age of Hollywood; many of her latex blouses, jackets, and dresses are named after glamour icons like Joan Crawford, Lana Turner, and Jean Harlow. Need something special for a wilder occasion? More adventurous shoppers can snap up waist cinchers, intricate latex masks, bra and hip cages, rubber masks with tiny perforations for breathing, and a straitjacket that inflates like a puffer fish.

The Baroness is tall and elegant with neon pink hair. When I met her for a French 75 cocktail at one of her favorite bars in the East Village, she wore a black silk blouse with gold printed skulls, a latex pencil skirt, stockings, and heels. She carries herself like, well, a baroness. She makes every seat she sits in look like a chaise longue. She is a total original, a mix of manners and minx.

"I didn't have a choice; it was my destiny. I came out of the womb an oddball," she told me. "I grew up in Britain, where everyone wore uniforms. Everything, including the lifestyle, was more conservative. I felt like people didn't want me to look too exotic or too interesting. But I dressed wildly. I rebelled against the norm.

"I've always felt very powerful, clothing-oriented to the point of obsession, pretty much unable to work for anyone else," she said. "And I've seen people literally drop to their knees because of how I look. I mean, that's the power of clothing."

The Baroness loves the freaky, the bizarre, the eccentric. She cannot bear the boring, the banal, and people who lack imagination. Anyone can wear latex, she said. The sizes in her shop go from XS to 2X. She believes that anyone who comes into her shop should understand that she'd never sell a customer a piece of her clothing that wouldn't make the person feel special.

"When a person comes into my shop and tells me that she's too fat to wear latex, I want to tell her to get the fuck out," she said. "It's insulting. Some people get an idea in their head of what they look good in. That's fine, but don't bring that energy into my store."

Anyone can put on a little black dress and feel pretty for a night out. But finding a style that projects your soul, that makes you feel like you own the room is something very different. Dressing to project your inner power means looking beyond the pages of magazines or your Instagram feed to gaze deep within yourself.

"If you don't know who you really are, if you don't have that strong foundation, then how the fuck can you exude anything?" said The Baroness. "How can you expect them to give you anything back?"

Before meeting her, I'd never thought about the difference between inviting the gaze of others and hoping they like what they see and projecting a style outward and demanding people accept me for who I am.

YOU MUST DRESS FOR TODAY

A few years ago, I found an envelope of old photos of myself in a shoebox. While looking through them, I was horrified to see that, with a few experimental exceptions, I had the same hairstyle from the ages of seventeen to thirty-seven. For two decades, I used a paddle brush to blow my dark brown hair straight and then I'd part it in the middle. True, in a daring move at around age twenty-six, I started parting it on the side. When hairstylists tried to convince me to cut choppy layers or give me a sleek bob, I'd go into a panic. No, I'd squeak! Just a trim!

I was definitely not the same person at thirty-seven that I was at seventeen. So why was I so afraid to change? What was it about that hairstyle that felt so safe and right? The answer was, after years of wrestling and agonizing through puberty, it was a style that finally worked for me. Long, straight hair made me feel cute at an age when I felt awkward about everything else.

"A lot of us keep a style that we came up with at the best time in our lives," said The Baroness. "That's how your style can become stagnant."

I know a guy who still dresses like he did in 1998. Baggy jeans, Timberlands, oversized sweaters, and puffy jackets. Twenty years later, his clothing makes him seem uncomfortable in the present. His clothing projects nostalgia for the nights he funneled beers at his frat house. Maybe that was the time in his life when *he* felt the best about himself. His Timberlands are something safe to hold on to, just like my stick-straight hairdo.

It's amazing how our closets can function as photo albums of our past.

The clothing that we amass tells the story of our lives. All the sweaters, T-shirts, and jeans crammed onto our shelves carry the weight of personal history. A pair of low-rise jeans you bought back in college may bring back memories of carefree nights out with your girlfriends back when all you had to worry about were hangovers and term papers. Your first "grown-up" handbag, the one that cost you half your first paycheck, may be battered and in need of repair but it still summons that new-in-the-city excitement, a feeling you haven't had for a long time. The bridesmaid's dress that you wore to your best friend's wedding five years ago may remind you of a happier time, back when the two of you were closer. You can't part with that ugly cardigan from your late grandmother because even though she's gone, you worry it would hurt her feelings.

"That's the power of clothing, because it really caters to your desire to be hugged and held," said The Baroness. "You may still have your First Communion dress and think, *I can't get rid of this because there's so much power from that day in that dress.* Plus you'd be like, *Oh no, I'm not throwing away God.*"

We keep our memories, the good and the bad, stuffed in our drawers. Parting with the past is scary because once it's gone you have to face the uncertainty of the future. When I culled my closet this year, I had to face a lot of hard truths about how I'd spent my money over the last five years. So many dresses, shirts, and skirts had been purchased on impulse to soothe whatever feelings of sadness or anxiety I was feeling that day. It was so easy to patch together bits and pieces of a wardrobe in the same way that I'd patched over all my feelings of uncertainty about my life.

Happily, not all of my clothing went into the Goodwill bin. To my surprise, amid the piles of cowl-necked sweaters, capri pants, velour sweatshirts, and pointy-toed high heels with toe cleavage (ugh) was evidence of a personal style. There were colorful wrap dresses, a few black blazers, and a leather bag that just needed a good polish. It turned out that I didn't have to throw it all away and start again. There were bits of fashion that made me feel good in there. I just had to toss away all of what wasn't working.

YOUR CLOTHING IS MAGICAL

When I met Mistress Couple for coffee in the Bushwick section of Brooklyn, my first impression was of a ballerina in tall black punk boots. Her long bleached blonde hair was pulled into a ponytail, the sides shaved into neat rows. When she was training to become a dominatrix, she was given the name Couple to honor her career as a ballroom dancer. There was much about the art of dancing with a partner that translated from the dance floor to the dungeon, she said. Someone leads, the other follows. Kink has its own beauty, grace, and choreography.

Mistress Couple told me that her training at the BDSM château La Domaine Esemar offered her the freedom to dress the way she wanted, to project her own personal brand of power.

"Back when I was working in the dance studio, it was frowned upon for the female instructors to wear pants or slacks. But pants are really what makes me feel sexy and comfortable," she said. "So it was very hard to feel empowered in my job when I felt like I was being objectified."

One night, after a student party, she found herself cleaning up champagne glasses while all the male instructors were laughing and screwing around in the ballroom.

"That was the first time Mistress Couple showed up," she said. "I went out and was like, 'No, you guys are gonna come back here and help me do this, I'm not doing this for you.' It was then that I slowly began to realize that my job was not serving me anymore."

Getting dressed in the morning is a push and pull to find that balance between what makes us feel good and what is considered professional.

"The dress code at La Domaine was whatever made you feel simultaneously comfortable and sexy," she said. "The com-

fortable part is the most important, because if you're not comfortable, you're not going to feel sexy."

In 2019, the idea of dressing sexy at work can set off alarm
bells for women. Harnessing your sexuality isn't the same as
dressing provocatively or showing a lot of skin, she said. Your
clothing doesn't have to be formfitting for it to radiate everything you love about yourself. It's the tying yourself to strict
ideas of what's "sexy" that can hold you back.

"For me, saying 'fuck you' to gender norms has been really
powerful in terms of exploring how to express myself with
clothes," said Mistress Couple.

What if you work in a bank, or need to wear a uniform?
If your paycheck depends on you wearing khaki slacks and a
name tag, this can all seem like a moot point. Mistress Couple's
advice? Choose a piece of clothing or an accessory that you can
put on in the morning that channels that "don't fuck with me"
feeling. Putting it on can feel like a ceremony, like you're pre-
paring for battle. A talisman, she said, is something that only
you know you're wearing and the power you've imbued it with.

"Wearing objects that hold powerful memories can help
during times when you feel powerless," she said.

A talisman can be a ring your grandmother gave you for
your high school graduation or a bracelet that your best friend
gave you when you swore that you'd be sisters for life. Just
like the items in your closet may hold negative memories of
your past, meaningful objects can be a lifeline to times in our
life when we were loved and felt like we were worthy. A talisman can alter your headspace and change the way you approach your work or any other situation where you need extra
strength.

"When I'm getting ready for sessions or I'm training someone for dominance, I tell them to always have one item that
they can use as a power talisman," she said. "The only thing

that matters is that when you put it on, you say and feel, 'Ah, there she is.'

"For me, it's my thigh-high boots. On some days, I don't really feel like Mistress Couple until the boots are on."

When a professional dominatrix dresses for work, every article of clothing she puts on has a purpose. She's dressing to project the kind of power that she knows will electrify (and perhaps terrify) a particular client. A corset that offers a peek at her cleavage is an excellent choice for cruel teasing. A pair of latex opera gloves projects icy sophistication. Leather boots with a three-inch platform and seven-inch heels will definitely inspire awe in a man who wants to worship a six-foot goddess. But she's not just dressing for the client. Her clothing can give her a jolt of confidence to get her through her workday.

"I love what Alexandria Ocasio-Cortez and Kyrsten Sinema are doing. They're just insisting on being themselves in what they wear," said Mistress Couple. "AOC wrote a tweet about how she was going to keep wearing her gold hoop earrings so that when girls in the Bronx get yelled at by their teachers to take out their hoops, they could say, 'No, I'm dressing like a congresswoman.'"

Ocasio-Cortez knows that a hoop earring isn't just any old piece of jewelry. It's a statement about urban Latina culture and feminine power. It's a signifier.

In 2017, Callia Hargrove, the former social media editor at *Teen Vogue*, told *Refinery29* style writer Bianca Nieves that "communities of color have *always* embraced [hoop earrings], but with an understanding that outside of the comforts of our communities and families, they are seen differently, in a negative light. Knowing that, wearing hoops in those settings almost feels like a form of activism."[2]

Gold hoops, red lipstick, colorful dresses that show off arm muscles. They're ways of exuding a feminine sexuality in a way that shows strength and power and that these women are not the same old do-nothing people in Washington.

"They're saying 'No, wearing a power suit and short hair doesn't make me feel powerful. Owning my femininity does,'" said Mistress Couple. "'And so screw you, I'm gonna wear what I want to wear.'"

What makes lingerie "sexy"? It depends on who it's for. I'm a lingerie person, but I like things that look modern and practical. I live in New York; I don't have the closet space for satin teddies, filmy peignoirs, and feather boas. I wear underwear for myself. If I feel sexy under my clothes, I'm going to project it outward, no matter what I'm wearing to work.

Clients may pay for a certain aesthetic (the Goth Queen, the Cruel Governess, the Mean Girl from High School), but in order for her to look and act commanding, she has to be comfortable in her skin. She does not have the time to be pulling or tugging, or worrying that she's popping out and giving away too much flesh to an unworthy subject. Mere mortals fret that their shapewear is crawling up their thighs and digging into their bellies.

A Goddess does not concern herself with Spanx.

"Your sexuality is such a source of creativity and power. It's remiss to leave it out," said The Baroness. "Even as a kid, I always liked to have my wrists bound with wide bracelets. It made me feel powerful. Like, I exist."

Your clothing can be a form of armor. It can protect you from outside forces that want to get inside you, to make you feel powerless. But armor can be heavy. It can be a burden, if you let it. Sometimes a leather jacket is just a jacket. Other times it's protection against the people around us who don't see us for who we are.

"I can take off my armor when I need to take it off, when I'm with certain friends or when I'm with my partner," said

Lucy Sweetkill. "And yeah, it would be great if I didn't have to wear armor, but the reality of living in this world is, I do.

"But instead of letting my armor weigh me down, I see it as part of my outfit."

Dressing for power is personal. It may change over time, and that's a good thing. The ring that kept bullies away as a teenager can serve you later as a reminder that you deserve more from a job or a relationship. In the end, clothing is just clothing. It's you that had the power all along.

"I GLITTER, I SHINE"

I remember when I was planning my wedding and wondering if I should invest in lingerie for the big night after the ceremony. Note: I'd been living with my husband for four years, so it wasn't going to be a big reveal. But what does "wedding night" lingerie even *mean*? I've attended bachelorette parties where "wedding night lingerie" meant something very specific. The Victoria's Secret bridal lingerie collection is lots of frills, lace, and bows. It's white; it's weirdly virginal, sort of like a "sexy angel" Halloween costume. I didn't want to be unwrapped like a present on my wedding night. I wanted to collapse on the hotel bed, kick off my shoes, and get to the hot sex.

I didn't buy any wedding lingerie but I did get suckered into buying sparkly white wedding shoes, which were both expensive, uncomfortable, and of course, can never be worn again. But I felt pressure to buy the dang shoes.

Resisting the desire to conform to fashion trends can feel futile. My Instagram barrages me with ads urging me to surrender and buy ballet flats and a romper. When I walk down the street, all the mannequins in the window mock me for eschewing high-waisted jeans. Fast fashion means that nothing is in style for long. Items go in and out of stores, they get marked down, they end up on the sale rack. There's always a new pattern, a new bit of lace put here or there, a paid celebrity influencer who shows up on the red carpet wearing a pair of bearskin gladiator sandals with four-inch platforms made of recycled Mountain Dew bottles.

You're not supposed to be able to keep up. It was such a relief when I finally realized I didn't have to.

I don't want to "get the look" of a celebrity. I want to showcase all the things I love about *myself.*

I don't want to be current. I want to be timeless.

"You want people to notice *you*, not your clothing," said The Baroness. "That's the point of personal style."

Dressing for power means having the confidence to shrug off trends. True fashion icons are icons because of their fierce commitment to their own style, not to every look that rolls off the runway. Rihanna, Madonna, Grace Jones, Audrey Hepburn, Michelle Obama, Marlene Dietrich—their clothing defines their image; it doesn't dictate it. It's all too easy to buy clothing from a certain brand and let it become our identity, rather than enhancing what we've already built.

Dia Domina Dynasty recommends making style rules for yourself and enforcing them.

"I find that sometimes people get caught up in the sizing of clothes and that the number size of your clothing dictates fitness. This is very untrue," she said. "So one rule I give myself is to disregard the number sizing of clothes and try them on no matter what."

We can't control how others see us, no matter how hard we try. What we can control is how we *feel* in our clothes. I have to be okay with giving up control over how others perceive me.

I can't force other people to see my worth, I can only use what I wear to beam out my best to the universe.

"When I show up somewhere, I can hardly get in a fucking room because my hair's big, my heels are big, my tiara's big. I glitter, I shine," said The Baroness. "But then people start to think I'm dressing for them. I'm not, and that's something that's hard for people to understand."

When I lived in Manhattan, I used to see this amazing older woman in the grocery store who pushed her cart around while decked out in tight leopard pants, enormous rhinestone sunglasses, and *two* fur coats. She treated that express checkout line like the red carpet at the Tony Awards and I loved it. She wasn't just making a statement; she *was* the statement. She was saying, *I'm fucking fabulous.* I'm not sure if all the other shoppers were receiving her message but I heard it loud and clear. Her furs were a little ratty and her handbag was stuffed with trash (I peeked), but she wanted the world to know that she may have fallen on hard times but she wasn't going to change for the bag boy or anyone else.

She wasn't a dominatrix but, looking back, she had domme energy.

Clothing says a lot about where you came from, who you are now, and what you stand for.

GET A WARDROBE THAT SERVES YOU

Think back to who gave you style advice when you were young. Now ask yourself, did they know what they were talking about? And if they did have wisdom to impart to you during your formative years, is it relevant to you now?

I'd always been told that I should only wear garments that were fitted at the waist, because it would accent my shape and make it look more pleasing. It wasn't bad advice, don't get me wrong. But dressing only to flatter one's figure can take a lot of the joy out of fashion. It's hard to feel powerful when you're sucking it all in and worried about how others are perceiving your silhouette.

One winter day, I wandered into Yeohlee Teng's shop on Twenty-Ninth Street with my in-laws. Yeohlee, a celebrated designer originally from Malaysia whose works are part of the permanent collection of the Costume Institute at the Metropolitan Museum of Art, selected a black raincoat for me to try on. On the hanger, it looked shapeless. Where were the darts? The belt? But after she convinced me to put it on (it was very expensive), I couldn't believe how great it looked. The material was light and airy, not at all like the heavy raincoats I'd owned in the past. I felt like a glamour witch on the cover of a Gothic novel. Then I thought about how I used to wish that I was thin enough to wear chic shapeless fashion instead of having to constantly worry about cinching in, about flattering my figure.

"Who told you that everything has to be fitted at the waist?" she asked me. "That's so old-fashioned."

I was missing out on the transformative magic of clothing, by sticking to the advice that Stacy London told me on an episode of *What Not to Wear* in 2006. I began to rethink.

My wardrobe should reflect the person I am now, not the person I'd be if I had a time machine or a different body. Every item, whether I paid five dollars or five hundred dollars for it, should make me feel like a queen.

So when I went through my closet, I held up each garment and asked myself the following questions:

- Does it make me feel good when I wear it?

- Can I dance in it?

- Can I laugh in it?

- Am I holding on to it for emotional and not practical reasons?

- Am I keeping it because I spent a lot of money on it?

- Am I holding on to it because I may "fit back into it one day"?

- Do I wear this or do I hide behind it?

- Is it itchy?

- Can I strike a pose in it?

- Do I feel sexy in it?

Again, I don't mistake "sexy" for showing a lot of skin or aimed at garnering attention from men. "Sexy" means I walk tall. It means I swagger. It means I buy the bigger size because I look fabulous in it. Sexy underwear is underwear that doesn't ride up or chafe my gentle areas. Any lingerie is sexy if it makes me want to dance around my bedroom and pose in front of the mirror.

Unless I am being carried to and from an event by a handsome manservant or being chauffeured by limo away from puddles and sewer grates (sadly, this has yet to happen), my shoes must be stylish, but also comfortable. Drag queens call it "stomping the runway," not "inching down the runway and then tripping and landing face-first in Anna Wintour's lap." When I first moved to the city, my father told me that I should wear shoes comfortable enough so that I can escape from an attacker. Fleeing predators aside, he had a point. If I can't walk in them, if they make me feel off-balance, I don't buy them.

The day I tossed my "fuck me" pumps in favor of "fuck

you" boots was exhilarating. I want to feel strong standing on my own two feet. In my fantasy, I use my boots to get to where I need to be on time and, if I need to, to kick an assaulter in the dick and then, after hitting him in the eyes with my pepper spray, I rest my boot heel on his writhing back. Then I casually dial the police, inform them that I've done their job for them, and to please come pick up the trash.

Do I have sweatpants and T-shirts that I got for free? Heck yeah, I want something comfy for rainy Sundays when I'm curled up on the couch watching old movies. But if the T-shirts aren't buttery soft, they get torn up to become rags or they go into the trash.

Before you look into your closet, take a look at yourself. What makes you feel like you can kick down a door or tell a catcaller to fuck off? Maybe it's workout clothes that show off your muscles. Maybe it's a pair of tall boots with tights and a leather jacket. It could be a kick-ass pair of jeans with a blazer or a studded belt. Whatever it is, whatever you put on, it must be the best, happiest version of yourself at that moment.

It's okay to keep clothing from the past, as long as it reflects the person you are today versus the person you were when you felt less powerful and sure of yourself.

There's nothing wrong with loving a certain style and sticking to it for life. The question you have to ask is "Am I still this person?" If the answer is "hell yeah" then keep it. All that matters is that you feel like you're putting your truest self out there.

Autumn Whitefield-Madrano, the beauty writer and author, told me that her idea of dressing for power isn't figuring out what others find attractive, but creating a closet that makes her feel energized.

"I used to have this knee-length denim circle skirt—it was plain to the point of frumpy, especially because I would wear it with loose T-shirts. But for whatever reason, I felt *sexy as hell* when I put it on," she said. "In no universe was this item of clothing erotic, but what I felt while wearing it was like a private little secret.

"Nobody else would know that I was feeling sexy in that moment, though perhaps when wearing it I radiated something I wouldn't have otherwise. That's what made it special, private, and mine alone."

That's magic.

"YOU PUT ON A GARMENT, AND YOU'RE DIFFERENT"

Consider the corset, the iconic piece of clothing most associated with dominatrixes. Why do they wear them? They're tight; they're constricting; they squish your organs. I associated corsets with the nineteenth century, when women, determined to achieve the ideal feminine figure, sipped tea, got the vapors, and then died from the arsenic in their wallpaper. Or, in their modern iterations, cheesy bedroom theater, something soft-core porny and costume-y to seduce your man.

When I told The Baroness I'd be attending DomCon in Los Angeles, she told me to stop by her booth and watch as customers tried on her clothing.

"You'll see how they change," she said. "They stand up straighter. They're more powerful."

Weeks later, at DomCon, I stood by her table and watched her carefully lay out each handmade garment. Latex doesn't look like much at first glance. It's flat, it's floppy, it's shapeless. When you hold a latex dress up against your body, it's hard to imagine it ever fitting an actual human.

I watched The Baroness usher a petite dominatrix with rockabilly bangs into the makeshift dressing room. "Try this one," she commanded, and handed her a black-and-white polka-dotted latex dress.

After much wrestling and pulling behind the curtain, the dominatrix emerged looking like a mix of Minnie Mouse and mermaid. I, along with several onlookers, oohed and aahed as she admired herself in the mirror.

But when The Baroness handed me a latex pencil skirt, I initially demurred. I didn't want to tell The Baroness that I, too, felt like I was "too fat for latex." I thought of what my parents would think, of how I might look like a fool exiting the dressing room. So many years of voices in my head saying *Um, you can't wear that* are hard to mute.

But then, I remembered what she said, that anyone can look good in latex. She handed me a bottle of body lubricant (yes, you have to lube up your body to get into latex) and I oiled up. I slid the slippery tube up over my hips and thighs. I walked out of the dressing room and saw myself in the mirror. I looked . . . good? No, I looked fucking hot. It was something the world's sexiest school mistress would wear. I had an urge to pick up a ruler and scare the shit out of a roomful of college boys.

Suddenly, I *got* it. The latex hugged me, it curved with me. It was so close to my skin, it felt like skin, but it was synthetic, rubber, airless, fetish-y. Latex is hard to get on, but it's also hard for a lover to take off. It radiates sex, but also untouchability. I was so close to being naked and yet I felt wrapped and protected. It was better than feeling desired, I felt that I was desire itself.

When I stepped out to show The Baroness that I had indeed managed to get it onto my body, she spun me around and wrapped one of her handmade waist cinchers around me and pulled the laces *tight*.

Suddenly, as she predicted, I was jolted up straighter. I went from good-natured reporter to Executrix. For the first time, I actually felt like the woman in my fantasies, the woman who enters the conference room and throws her bag down on the table and says, "Listen up, assholes. Things are about to change around here."

"People assume you're not to be fucked with, because you look like you're not to be fucked with," said The Baroness.

"You walk into a place and people think you're somebody. They think they need to do things for you," she said. "Why do they do this? Because of how you look."

When I walked around the hotel, I felt people looking at me differently. I got into an elevator full of men in suits and they stopped talking. I felt the energy shift my way. They all moved out of the way for me and we rode up in complete silence. I didn't smile once. Why should I have?

"And what did you do?" The Baroness asked, triumphantly. "You just got dressed."

YOU HOLD YOUR OWN

SEXUAL POWER

Once you have a handle on loving yourself, you
can practice sharing that love with others.

—JANET W. HARDY AND DOSSIE EASTON

Let's face it. We all have moments when we look at ourselves naked in the bathroom mirror and think, *Yeah, I'd fuck me.* When there's no one else around to pass judgment on our looks, we can be free to feel as gorgeous as we want. After all, there's no need to bother with another person when we've got so much sexual energy burning inside us.

There's an art to feeling sexy when you're all by yourself. Think of all the things that touch your body every day: your shirt, your perfume, your jeans, your deodorant, your jewelry. Imagine if we stopped to process the pleasure we receive from all the ways we touch our bodies each day.

Objects that make me feel sexy and powerful include: red lipstick, exotic perfume, heavy bracelets, wrap dresses, and the magical combination knee-high boots and opaque tights. I haven't had a cigarette in years, but holding one between my fingers used to make me feel wicked. Objects are just objects until we put them on our bodies and make them come alive. But in my hand, on my body, on my wrists, or on my lips, they give me a full-body erotic *zing*.

Can books make you feel sexy? Reading a book on the subway is a little kinky, because people are watching me enjoy something alone. Laughing gives me enormous pleasure. There's no more earth-shattering orgy than the sound of an entire roomful of people laughing together at the same joke. Sometimes doing my laundry can feel sexy, because yeah, I'm touching intimate objects, the room is warm and smells good. I feel like a haughty queen when I dine alone or when I lean in close so a friend can share a secret with me. Don't get me wrong, I like hanging out with other people. But there's nothing as delightful as enjoying my own company.

That's why it's so jarring when a dude tries to chat me up when I'm feeling myself. My sex vibe has nothing to do with anyone else. I may be in a beautiful dress, but when I'm walking down the street, I'm on my own cloud. Is there anything more annoying than a guy asking you to take out your headphones when you're listening to a beautiful song to ask you what you're reading? It's not flattering. It's disruptive. Stop trying to stick your boner into our self-contained feeling of joy, guy.

Also, no, I don't feel like a luminous sex goddess every day. Most mornings, I wake up with crust in my eyes, drool on my pillow, and crumbs on my nightshirt. It takes time to psych myself up for the day, to get dressed, to put on makeup, to find that special something that gives me that little boost. And even if I've given myself the time to make myself feel good, it doesn't always come together. I asked one of my friends with little kids about her morning beauty ritual and she laughed in my face. For many of us, getting our teeth brushed and our hair combed before we run out of the house for work is the big glamour victory of the day.

Even Alpha women get the blues. Professional domina-trixes also wake up with crust in their eyes and pillow creases on their faces. She has to summon her own energy before sessions. She's got to be the divine feminine, even if she doesn't feel all that divine that day. Even if her client believes that she's a goddess, she's got to search within herself to find that light.

Locating your sexuality amid the rubble of your everyday sadnesses, anxieties, and fears takes practice.

LEARN TO (LITERALLY) FEEL YOURSELF

Let's talk sensual pleasure. We're so busy trying to look good for others that we forget to enjoy the little things we do every day, the rituals.

Even if you're not super into serums, yoga, candles, and gratitude journals, there's deep solitary joy in taking time for yourself.

Self-care may feel decadent and wasteful. It can run counter to the reality of our budgets, the woes of the world, and the fact that there are only so many hours in the day. If you're a new mom, juggling multiple jobs, or barely making ends meet, allocating time and money to self-worship is a fantasy. Still, there's so much to be mined from even the most mundane daily rituals.

Our days are full of sensual pleasures that we take for granted. Hot showers feel amazing; scrubbing our backs with a loofah is delicious. Rubbing lotion on our legs is incredibly intimate—working it into our calves, behind our knees, and all over our thighs. Come on, we've all been walking around with delicious-smelling legs and the world doesn't even know it! That's an incredibly sexy sensual secret.

"I actually love shaving my legs," said Autumn Whitefield-

Madrano. "Now, I don't actually *like* shaving my legs. For a while I just stopped shaving during the winter. But I found that it instantly plummeted how sensuous I felt, even if nobody was going to be seeing or touching my legs," she said.

"The ritual of shaving—of taking time to work with the curves of my legs—may have been instilled in me due to patriarchal bullshit standards. But if the end result is something that puts me in touch with my favorite part of my body every time I shower, then at this point in my life, I'm okay with it."

My God, when was the last time you got naked and spread yourself out on your bed and felt the fan blow on your damp summer skin? To stretch out, wiggle your toes, take three deep breaths in and out, and suddenly be at peace for a few moments. That feeling is all yours.

Sensual power is about feeling yourself when there's no one else around. It's taking time to appreciate your skin, your muscles; to revel in all of your senses.

Have you ever smelled the inside of your shirt during the day and thought to yourself, *Damn, that's good*? Because I have. Sometimes, I'll put perfume on before I go to bed at night because it helps me relax and get myself in the mood for a good night's sleep or nighttime endeavors. Much like myself, my choice in fragrances has evolved over the years. I used to like scents that were light, lemony, and sweet. Now I like to smell dark, spicy, and a little intimidating. Tom Ford's unisex scent Ombre Leather evokes the scent of riding on the back of a beautiful woman's motorcycle. It's aggressive, oily, a little dirty, a little sweet, and it makes me feel very, very sexy. It's off-putting in the best way. A straight male friend of mine said it smelled "confusing." Clearly, it was doing its job.

In old Hollywood movies, ladies sit in front of their mirrors with dreamy expressions on their faces, slowly brushing their hair, a hundred strokes a night. I imagine they're feeling soft bristles against their scalp, an erotic stimulation of nerve endings masquerading as an ordinary task. We, too, can dab lip balm on our mouths, stroke our earlobes before we slide earrings in, inch (not yank) our stockings over our legs and revel in the soft pressure of sheer fabric curving against our hips and thighs. That's why opaque tights are so sexy; they show off our legs without allowing anyone to see what's underneath.

It reminded me of what The Baroness said about wearing latex. "I can feel it touching me all day. I feel it when I walk, when I sit, when I cross my legs. It's touching me but you can't."

■ ■ ■

All of this internalized sexual power has potent effects on people around us. Have you ever watched a confident woman walk into a restaurant and felt the whole vibe of the room change? She doesn't have to acknowledge the impact that her scent, her style, and her energy are having on us. It's all about *her*. She's holding the moment and reveling in it. Because it's often way hotter (and feels way more powerful) to accept the attraction and hold it, rather than feel pressure to engage.

"I feel sexiest (as opposed to most turned-on) when I am in that moment of attraction—of feeling attracted to someone and perceiving that it's mutual. Hell, it doesn't even have to actually be mutual as long as it feels like it," Whitefield-Madrano said. "I'm happily monogamous, so I know that these moments won't lead to anything physical or explicit. But none of that is a factor, because it's just about the frisson of the moment and appreciating it."

If you've got kids or you share a bathroom with a partner or roommates, taking time for any kind of solo sensual ritual can be tough. But we all need to find time once in a while to connect and own all the beautiful things about ourselves. No one will ever love us like we do.

Every day, our bodies are out in the world. We share them with our lovers, our children, commuters on mass transit, and strangers in crowded elevators. Everyone wants a piece of us. We deserve to keep the best for ourselves.

YOU'RE THE LOVER WHO KNOWS YOU BEST

If you were ever a small child who liked to stuff pillows, teddy bears, or whatever else down into your underwear, chances are an adult came over and told you to cut it out.

It's so bad, it feels so good; it's so bad, it feels even better. The more our parents, our religions, our teachers, or our peers told us that it was wrong, weird, or filthy, the more thrilling (but also shaming) it all was. Experiencing pleasure when we're alone may bring back those feelings of self-loathing. This can manifest in a few different directions; we might never feel comfortable venturing south solo again, or we might dive in to ourselves with a vengeance.

Masturbating is the world's least secret shame. Literally, as you're reading this book, you are surrounded by hundreds of masturbators in your neighborhood, buzzing, jerking it, and writhing in self-induced ecstasy. If only we could harness the energy of all humanity's furtive stroke artists, we could cut down on coal emissions. Okay, that's probably not true, but I'm sure Elon Musk has at least considered the possibility.

I'm a Jewish woman, and therefore I didn't grow up with the kind of sexual guilt that a lot of my friends of other religions were dealt. I used to joke that I didn't have sex guilt, but

I had family guilt. Which meant I felt okay about sex, but I worried my deceased relatives were watching me and feeling extremely disgusted and disappointed.

I grew up in the 1990s, when everyone was talking about HIV/AIDS and people were talking seriously about safe sex and condoms. (They never talked about herpes and HPV, of course, but that's another book.) In high school, I felt like a self-conscious, sex-obsessed weirdo. I had boyfriends, but with the exception of a few sweet ones, they were all hands and no brains. The pressure to have sex was crushing. Masturbation was a way to cope with my own hormones without having to physically and emotionally wrestle with pushy boys who always wanted to go too far and too fast, with no thought to my feelings.

Unlike Brianna Rader, the founder of the sex counseling site Juicebox, I was lucky to have at least some sex education, if you could call it that. My health teacher (who was also the driver's ed teacher) made us watch as he struggled to put a condom on a banana and referred to masturbating as "choking the chicken." I remember when a boy in my class summoned up the courage to ask about anal sex, and my teacher asked if he was "looking to take a trip down the ol' Hershey highway?" Ultimately, I learned about sex the same way many from my generation did: from dirty books and HBO. I knew that sex would be great if I could just find a wonderful person to do it with. But in the meantime, doing it alone seemed like a safe and, frankly, more introspective alternative.

I couldn't have known it at the time, but all that time alone, reading, thinking, dreaming, and getting off, was actually laying the foundation for a positive sexual future. As a teenager who longed to grow up and move to the city, all the writers and filmmakers I adored, like Todd Haynes, Tama Janowitz, and Lynda Barry, had complicated and out-there ideas about sex. My Sweet Valley High books had romance but it wasn't my idea of sexy.

The 1990s weren't all that enlightened. I remember in 1994, the US surgeon general was ousted for daring to promote masturbation as a safe alternative to sex. Sexual self-exploration wasn't something that I could just casually mention to my female friends during a commercial break during *The Real World*. They already thought I was odd for liking movies with subtitles. I just added it to the pile of all the other activities I secretly enjoyed that I assumed were gross, weird, antisocial, and freakish.

Now you can buy a vibrator at CVS.com, and you can throw a "cock ring" along with razor blades and vitamins into your virtual cart when you shop online at Walmart! And when you get your new toys home, you don't even need batteries; you can charge them with a USB cable or connect them to your phone via Bluetooth. There are so many sex toys for women, aimed at pleasuring so many parts of our vaginas, that it's an embarrassment of riches. But being able to march into a well-lit, female-focused sex toy shop and walk out with a $125 G-spot stimulator with clitoral attachments is the easy part. Untangling the feelings that keep our arousal elusive is a harder nut to crack. And the more mainstream vibrators and sex toys become, the more we feel like idiots for not knowing what to use or how to achieve orgasm. It's anxiety on top of anxiety.

Searching for your pleasure can be a lonely endeavor. A kind and patient partner can help, but if you're all tied up inside and arousal feels like another task you can't accomplish, it's going to be a slog.

"When I started at La Domaine Esemar, I would meet women who said, 'I don't know how to have an orgasm.' Or 'It's really hard for me to,'" said Mistress Couple. "Then somebody would ask them, 'Do you masturbate?' And the answer was usually no, or they've only tried one particular thing and they don't know what else to do."

How can we experience solo or mutual pleasure if we're grappling with the idea that we shouldn't be doing it in the first place? You're untangling two complex knots at once. If you're still hearing the same judgmental voices in your head that tormented you back in your teenage years, you may want to consider talking to a therapist before investing more money in toys that will gather dust on your night table.

Finding out what gets you going isn't the same as finding the perfect productivity software or pair of heels you can walk in. You're searching for self-gratification but you may also be trying to make a sexual relationship with a partner more fulfilling. How can we direct our lovers when we're still clueless about how to solve our own internal mysteries? Solving for both of those sexual conundrums takes longer than reading the instructions on how to operate your Relentless Vibrations Remote Control Ecstasy Egg. But you owe it to yourself to try.

NO ONE CAN "MAKE YOU COME"

This may come as a shock to those who claim to have magic dicks or wizard tongues, but no one person can "make you come." Hot sex isn't like putting together IKEA furniture. It takes more than screws, sweat, and two people awkwardly matching up parts to make it work.

Anyone who makes the bogus claim that they can "give you an orgasm" doesn't understand how female orgasms work. An orgasm comes from within us; it can't be gifted like a fruit basket. You have to feel aroused, in the mood, ready to receive pleasure, and hungry for it. If the mind isn't feeling it, the soul and body won't either. Your lover can throw you every move under the sun, but if you're not feeling it, chances are you're just not going to get there. Your sexual arousal and orgasm are yours to experience, not someone else's to give.

This may frustrate our partners, especially if they've cracked their knuckles and are hell-bent on "making you come." Our lovers can mean well, but they can also miss the point.

I really liked what Vanessa Marin, a sex therapist and creator of the online orgasm course Finishing School, told Anna Fitzpatrick of *Vice* in 2017 about handling partners who approach your orgasm with the blind, competitive determination of someone stalking a Pokémon.[1]

"A lot of my clients will tell me, 'I'll be with somebody who's really going over the top about wanting to make me orgasm, and it feels more like he wants to do it to make himself feel good and feel like he's gotten a gold star rather than because he genuinely cares about my experience," she told *Vice*. "This blows, and not in the sexy way. If you instead chill out a little and approach sex like an enjoyable activity that can be done with another person (or people), everyone involved will have a much better time."

A 2017 study published in the *Journal of Sex Research* found that men "felt more masculine and reported high sexual esteem when they imagined a woman orgasmed during sexual encounters with them, and that this was exacerbated for men with high masculine gender role stress. These results suggest that women's orgasms do function—at least in part—as a masculinity achievement for men."[2]

When we fake orgasms, we're giving up all our sexual power, but not in the way you may think. We all know that you don't need to have an orgasm to have a delicious and intimate night with a lover. But by feeling pressure to have an orgasm and then solving that by faking it, we're being forced from our own headspace to become a caretaker for someone else's fragile ego. It also means that we don't feel comfortable communicating that we're having a lovely time, but it's just not happening tonight. It's hard to relax when you're scrambling to figure out what's wrong and how we can fix it so our partner feels okay about it.

By approaching your orgasm and your pleasure as your possession, you can start communicating with your partner about how things are going to go. "Honey, I may not come every time, that's just not how it works. But I really like being intimate with you and I get a lot of pleasure from the touching, the kissing, the feeling of being desired. Me not being an orgasm machine has nothing to do with how hot a lover you are and how great you are in bed."

When you realize that you are the one who holds your own sexual power, it all becomes a lot clearer. Your lover can bring the piñata to the party, but you, my friend, are the party itself.

An orgasm is the cherry on top of sex, but the cherry alone does not a sundae make. Great sex is about full body and mind connection. That's the part that takes effort. If "making you come" is all your partner is shooting for, it's kind of a low bar.

Instead, think of masturbation in the same context as other sensual pleasures. You can enjoy a steamy bubble bath without orgasm, but that doesn't ruin the pleasure of the experience. There's a whole world of sensation that you can enjoy before you have to worry about orgasm. There's a lot you can learn from spending time with your filthiest thoughts without worrying that you're not "getting there."

At the same time, there could be reasons why you're struggling that aren't in your head. Maybe you're taking a certain medication that's affecting your ability to climax. Maybe you're using the wrong vibrator (there's no return policy). Not everyone likes the same kind of back massage; why would you think you'd like the same "massager" as everyone else?

Trying can be trying. Just go easy on yourself. Your pleasure is worth pursuing. Start by giving yourself time to think about what turns you on. Touch other parts of your body. Embrace other aspects of your body's sensuality and ask yourself the hard questions. What's really on your mind when you're trying to get there? No $200 fifteen-speed swivel-head vibrator can help you achieve full understanding and acceptance of your thoughts and fears.

EXPLORE SELFLESS PLEASURE

You can also take a break from fretting and focus on pleasurable things that have nothing to do with sex and sensuality. Doing nice things for others (which is different from "people-pleasing") can give you a rush. You can use your power for good, and then enjoy the sensation of being appreciated, and making the world a slightly less shitty place.

Self-love and self-care aren't the same as being selfish. Spending time to figure out what brings you peace and pleasure isn't being narcissistic (as long as you're not hurting others). Being kind to others is a form of self-love. I've always felt better giving a gift than receiving one. That may be tied up in my feelings of self-worth and what I deserve, but there's nothing confusing about the joy I feel in surprising a friend with flowers or giving a friend who's down in the dumps a hug and pep talk.

I've used my body to make a moment of someone's life easier by holding a door for a parent struggling with a toddler and a stroller and felt joy upon receiving a grateful smile. Giving up my seat on the subway to an elderly person doesn't get me off, but it makes me feel good.

This can mean cooking a wonderful meal for you and a friend, or just for yourself. It can mean taking a walk to a part of town you haven't been to for a while, or calling a grandparent who may miss you. I'm not suggesting that emceeing bingo at your local retirement home is a reasonable substitution for satisfying sex, but I can nearly guarantee you'll feel better afterward than you would had you stayed in bed, feeling rotten about life. It's okay to feel good about having done good.

"If you have a hard time feeling valuable when no one is around to tell you that you are, then why not do something that is valuable to others?" write Janet W. Hardy and Dossie Easton in their bestselling book *The Ethical Slut*.[3] "Many unhappy sluts with no date this weekend have gone off to serve dinner to the homeless at a local church and come back filled to the brim with good feeling about all the pleasure they were able to give."

■ ■ ■

"When we learn to recognize and welcome love as we find it in our hearts and in all of its many and marvelous manifestations—sexual love, friendly love, passionate love, gentle love, overwhelming love, care taking love, and millions of others—we can discover a river of nourishment that can flow through our lives in a constantly replenishing stream. . . . Once you have a handle on loving yourself, you can practice sharing that love with others," write Hardy and Easton.

Start thinking about *all* the things that make you feel alive, both in and out of bed. Stop compartmentalizing your pleasure and let it all seep into other aspects of your life.

Once you know how and why you feel good, you'll feel more empowered to keep exploring—and then ask and receive more from yourself and others.

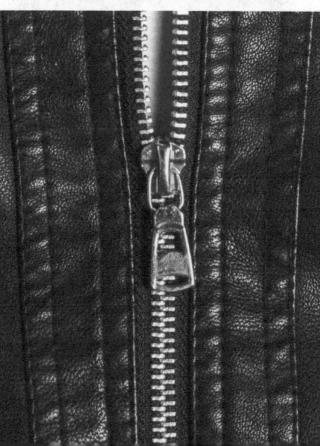

THE POWER OF
DESIRE

LESSON #10

YOU CAN DOMINATE
IN THE BEDROOM

If a woman has never had the experience of standing over her partner and being like, "I'm calling the shots," I highly recommend it.

—TINA HORN

Before we go any further, I want to talk about labels. Every pro-domme I spoke to advised me to tell you not to worry about them. Getting too attached to words like "submissive," "dominant," "tops," and "bottoms" can box us in rather than give us the freedom to explore. I know what I like in bed and I'm not afraid to ask for it, but I wouldn't call myself dominant, because I like different things according to what mood I'm in. I'm a complex carbohydrate. We all are.

If you want to get more into the BDSM lifestyle and dig deeper into rituals and the psychology, go for it. But for most of us, as we're wading in slowly, there's no need to categorize ourselves.

Before we get into all the ways we can play with exchanging power in bed, let's talk about *why* people enjoy exchanging power in bed.

The short answer is: It's hot as hell. For the long answer, keep on readin'.

WHY IS DOMINATING ANOTHER PERSON SEXY?

Not all of us have leadership roles at work, but at some point, we've given an order. We've told someone where to sit, where to hang their coat, to stop talking and listen. We've told someone where to meet us, and to please be on time. We've asked people to bring napkins to our parties, to pick up groceries on the way home, to turn down the thermostat.

You may not consider yourself a sexually dominant person, but you've probably made things happen by asking for what you want. Have you ever texted someone "come over tonight ;)" and had them show up at your door ten minutes later? Said "kiss me" and then found yourself kissed? Ordered someone not to stop doing something to you that felt wonderful? Pulled someone into a dark corner and made out with them? If you ever said "Fuck me now" to a lover, I can nearly guarantee that he or she didn't say "Quit bossing me around!" (If they did, I hope you dumped them.) More likely, he or she said "Yes, ma'am," and leapt to it.

We know this feeling, and it's good! Yet the idea of being a dominant female in the bedroom still seems strange. Besides bringing up a lot of preconceived gender notions about who should be steering the sex ship, it can sound intimidating. In the movies, either the sex is led by the dude or else it's this magically equal exchange. Even if the woman says "fuck me," the guy seems to be the one leading the fucking.

It's interesting that we feel more comfortable saying "Fuck me" versus "I'm going to fuck you." They're just words, and yet the latter seems to reveal something deeper and more transgressive.

Let's take a step back from sex and talk about how much we secretly admire and idolize dominant women. Don't we all long for a tough-but-fair female boss to teach us how to get what we want from a roomful of men? Don't we want to be that woman who walks into a room and strides past everyone without smiling or apologizing? I've always had the hardest girl-crushes on these kinds of smart, confident women. My whole life, I've had domme envy, I just hadn't known what to call it.

"Strip away the corny SM stereotype, and what you have is a femme in possession of power, sensuality, and most importantly, herself," writes Midori, a sexologist and founder of ForteFemme: Women's Dominance Intensive.[1] "She gracefully faces the obstacles and challenges of everyday life with humor and determination, and creates her own success and destiny."

We tweet and fangirl out on famous women who radiate sexual power in a way that says, "You can't handle all this." Why else do we admire singers like Nicki Minaj, Cardi B, Beyoncé, Dolly Parton, Tina Turner, and Joan Jett? Because they're divas. They get what they want. They suffer trials and tribulations in their personal lives, but still they rise and reign. We all want to be unstoppable forces. We all want to take what's ours.

My favorite dominant women in popular culture have always been the female villains. In *Game of Thrones*, Cersei Lannister may have been a pretty rotten person who killed a lot of innocent people, but blowing up the Great Sept with all her enemies inside was a serious power move. I love stories when women get to take revenge. Give me *Kill Bill*, *Carrie*, *Thelma & Louise*, *Bound*, and *The Craft* over *The Notebook* any day. My favorite movies are the ones where the femme fatale gets away with it, rather than being punished for her misdeeds. The female villain is always more interesting than the innocent heroine. I always thought Disney movies were boring. You can keep Ariel from *The Little Mermaid*; I'll hang with Ursula any day of the week.

If you bought this book, you probably want to know how to make your lover bow down and do your bidding. You just don't know how to make it happen. And if it *did* happen, what the heck to do next.

Taking the lead in bed doesn't mean being a sadist or demeaning your partner. It doesn't mean you have to change who you are. Think back to the chapter about your alter ego. You're simply connecting with a powerful side of yourself that was always there, and sharing it with a person who wants to make you happy.

WHY ARE WE AFRAID TO DOMINATE IN BED?

That's an easy one. We don't give ourselves credit for the amazing things we do every day. We have trouble accepting compliments. We play down our accomplishments out of fear of sounding "full of ourselves." Powerful women who take pride in their achievements get slapped down for not being modest or self-effacing.

We're expected to say "It's an honor just to be nominated" instead of "I won, and goddamn it, I deserved it."

We love the idea of being sexually catered to, but if we can't accept a compliment without feeling awkward, then a night of unreciprocated oral sex can feel very foreign.

In their work, pro-dommes may identify as sadists, as Mistresses, as Goddesses, as Queens, as Governesses. They may do wicked things, but will never hurt or abuse anyone without their consent. The best ones tap into their true natures to find the way they were meant to dominate.

"All of these things that I thought of as dominant traits like arrogance, and being mean, and being domineering and controlling, and all of these things. Abusing your power. Using it to manipulate people," said Mistress Couple. "None of those things are embodied by my dominance."

A lot of the things we've been taught about what makes sex hot and daring can actually limit your idea of what sex can actually be. So much of what gets bucketed into "foreplay" can be just as exciting and sensual as intercourse. Of course we deserve to experience all the orgasms. But we leave so much on the table when we let it take center stage to the rest of our pleasure.

Women are also afraid to be selfish in bed. It goes against everything we're taught. We must be fair, things must be equal, we must take care of the other person, we must make sure everyone else's needs are met before ours. But deep down, don't we long to have *our* needs met and not have to reciprocate, to just lie back and enjoy sex without guilt?

Kink is about the pleasures of the mind, not a race to see who comes first. Why do you have to give your partner an orgasm just because you've experienced one? Why must it always be a tie score? It can feel transactional. And that's boring. What if we didn't have to give so much all the time? What if we didn't have to share our toys?

Want to start experimenting with taking on a more dominant role in the bedroom? Try this. Say to your lover, "Do you know what I'd love tonight? If you could just go down on me." Or "This [whatever it is] is what I want to do tonight."

Men have no qualms about demanding what they want in bed. So why should you? If you've ever given your partner an orgasm just to make him happy and grateful, then asking for the same should make total sense. There's always the next time in bed. There's always more fun to be negotiated.

You're feeling good because you got to experience the kind of pleasure you wanted, and your partner feels good because, hey, he just rocked your world. He accomplished something. He did good. You can both fall asleep happy.

■ ■ ■

Here's something else. Just "being on top" isn't a power position unless you know why you're there and what you're getting out of it. Otherwise, you're just doing all the work, giving the pleasure, and providing a nice view to boot. But when you're on top from a place of wanting to take what's yours, to set the pace, get the pressure you want against your G-spot and clit, to control when he gets to come, to steer the whole ship, then you're onto something.

Taking a dominant role in bed means asking yourself why you've done things the same old way and then daring yourself to change it up. It means you hold the script.

"For women, it can be something as simple as deciding what things interest them," said Hudsy Hawn. "I will say this: My inner submissive usually always caters to my partner's kinks. That's the submissive in me wanting to please and be mothering, but at the same time, I *am* dominant because I know what I want.

"You have to figure out what, as a powerful woman, speaks to you as a goddess, and then how do you parlay that with your partner?"

You can stay true to your desires and your nature while still getting what you want. Just start by asking for one thing. Start by saying "I want."

RETHINK THE IDEA OF MALE SUBMISSION

I feel terrible that I cannot remember the comedian who made this joke, but it has always stayed with me.

"I get bummed out," the guy said. "Whenever girls post a picture of themselves wearing a new dress or a new shade of lipstick, all their friends go crazy, leaving comments like 'Gorgeous! You're amazing! Get it! Look at you, you sexy thing!' I bought a new shirt, I really liked it. I posted a photo of myself wearing it. I got no likes and one comment from my best friend from high school. He wrote one word: 'Gay.'"

It wasn't funny because the comedian was making light of homophobia (believe me, many comics rely on offensive terms instead of writing good jokes). It was just so pathetic. What a fucking world that a guy can't post a photo of himself in a T-shirt without immediately having his "manhood" questioned.

I'm not crying kegs of tears for straight men, but in many ways, they get a raw deal (stay with me). Showing vulnerability is still considered "weak." Boys are trained from an early age to stop crying and act "like a man." A man who shows emotion is shouted down by his peers for "acting like a little bitch." The only times I see men being lauded for crying are at a funeral and immediately after having won an NBA final. No wonder so many men in power seek out the services of pro-dommes. Only there, in secret, can they give up control, shed the weight of their responsibilities and the burden that comes from always having to feel like they're in charge.

What straight men say they want and what they secretly desire are two different things. In Lehmiller's survey of women and men, which was approximately 72 percent heterosexual, two-thirds had fantasized about receiving anal sex. Over half the male-identified respondents said they'd given some thought to the idea of receiving anal sex or pegging.

"This tells me a lot about how many men are turned on by pegging, or at least at the idea of p-spot (prostate) stimulation," wrote Lehmiller. "Some may interpret this data to mean that straight men aren't as straight as they claim to be."

Or at least that they're a lot more open to different kinds of pleasures than society says they're supposed to enjoy. I don't think being "straight" has anything to do with it. It's about the fun of it, the transgression, and duh, how it feels. Being led, controlled, and "forced" to be "bad" is well, hot.

Pro-dommes are the first to scoff at the idea that all men enjoy being dominant in bed and all women enjoy being submissive. They see firsthand that a lot of men long to be taken out of the driver's seat. If only these men took that self-knowledge out of the dungeon and acted more empathetically to the rest of the world! But no, once the session is over, many of them return home to their wives and jobs, until they have a chance to see a pro-domme again and get relief.

And what's so great about a dominant lover anyway?

Truth, most straight guys have no clue what that word really means, at least in a BDSM context. I'm relying on anecdotal evidence here (my friends, stories I've read on social media, my own experiences being a woman), but there are a lot of men out there who think they're being "dominant" when really, they're piss-poor lovers. Spanking a woman, telling her she's a dirty little slut, and jackhammering her for three minutes until he shoots it is not kinky sex. It's just bad sex.

That kind of sexual behavior gives kink a bad name. Because BDSM isn't just about controlling the other person. It's about power exchange. It's a give-and-take. It's a consensual exploration of the mind, not just an exercise for the genitals.

Women may say that they want their men to be more vulnerable, but do they? Most of my female friends balked at the idea of their partners taking on a "submissive" role in the bedroom.

"Women are just as likely as men to have such a big patriarchal idea that a man is supposed to be 'the man' in bed," said Tina Horn. "They think he's the one that's supposed to initiate, that he's not a real man unless he really wants to pound a woman."

This is how people end up getting in bed with preconceived notions of who they are and what they're supposed to do. No one is being their true selves or sharing the things that really get them off. We're all holding ourselves and others to the wrong standards.

"Sometimes men have fantasies about gender transgression because it's an available metaphor for what they really want, which is to feel submissive or to feel owned or to feel possessed or to feel like they're not the partner that has to be assertive or take all the responsibility or be the most energetic or be the doer," said Tina Horn.

Look, there are a lot of men out there who wear women's panties to work. I've seen hundreds of photos on fetish sites. It's their thing. And why not? Women's underwear feels great! But it's got to be a secret. And sometimes, that's the thrill. No one knows he's wearing it. He's doing it because it's so subversive, so naughty, so wrong. It feels wonderful. It feels true to him. It makes him feel a certain way that brings him pleasure. It's kinky. It's hot.

It's great to have kinky secrets until we wish they didn't have to be secrets. We all contain multitudes, and yet we're constantly told that if we venture outside of our lanes, we're abnormal.

Society (or pornography) accepts that a woman can enjoy submission, that she may enjoy calling her partner "daddy" and feeling turned on by being treated like a sex object. But if a straight man says that he wants to be ordered around, told what to do, and objectified, then he's something less than a man. That's ridiculous.

Maybe instead of thinking of him as "submissive" he may just be a lover who's more interested in your pleasure than in his own. And that can seem foreign to most of us, since we've become inured to the care and maintenance of dicks since our teenage years. From a young age, we're made to feel that no boner can be left behind.

Hey, Lindsay's tenth-grade boyfriend: Women feel just as shitty after being left hanging and unsatisfied as you do. But we didn't have the words for it. Guys got "blue balls," and we were guilted into healing this tragic malady. Never mind our own frustration and irritation.

As progressive as we all think we are, we're still caught in these gender traps. Or we do one thing in the bedroom, then talk a different game when we're out with our friends and family. I once heard a man describe another man who stayed home and took care of the kids while his wife worked at a hedge fund as a "beta."

I haven't read my Aldous Huxley in a while, but I can tell you, that's some deep, dark shit.

Women who like to take charge are accused of "wanting to be the man" or "having penis envy." Getting married in pants is still, in 2019, a shocking thing for a straight woman to do. A woman who makes more money than her husband (and about 38 percent[2] of them do) has to worry that her husband may feel resentful and emasculated. What if she dares to take it a step further and explore the power she enjoys at work in her bedroom?

No wonder we just jump in bed and keep our desires to ourselves.

"I've seen this a lot in my work as a sex therapist, that it can be the man who's swallowed the patriarchal Kool-Aid, and he's afraid that if his wife knew he was submissive she wouldn't think he was a man anymore," said Gloria Brame. "And sometimes, they're proven right. Some wives can demonize husbands over their sexual submission because that's an easy target. It can be a symbol for a lot of other things that could be wrong in the relationship."

Yes, men have to get over their ingrained ideas about power in the bedroom if they want to express their desire to make you the center of their world. But we also need to ditch those same notions to get comfortable with the idea that a guy gets off on giving you pleasure.

"There's nothing my partner loves more than giving me exactly what I want," said Mistress Ava Zhang. "He says that one of the greatest things he appreciates about our dynamic is I'm so crystal clear about what I want from him at all times, and what I don't want."

Let's all agree to shed the gender bullshit and embrace different kinds of feelings and sensations. Because some things that seem wrong can just feel, well, *right*. Accepting vulnerability from our partners is the only way to forge real connection. Otherwise we're just fucking into the void, going through the motions.

You never know what feels good until you ask for it. But you have to be just as ready to listen when your partner asks for what he or she wants in return.

"For any person to take on a dominant role in the bedroom is having someone, essentially, show you their belly. That is not to be taken lightly," said Tina Horn. "That person is choosing to say, 'I want to be vulnerable with you. I want you to do what you want with me. I trust you with my safety and my life. These are my boundaries and I trust that you will remember them and be mindful of them in the middle of a really hot, sexy moment. And I will go to wherever you tell me to go because I trust that space you are in is safe.'"

Exploring submission with your partner is allowing yourself to receive pleasure and to appreciate a partner who gets off on giving it to you.

"When I finally had a male submissive in my life, I was

so impressed," said Hudsy Hawn. "These guys are so much stronger and braver than your average middle-of-the-road, straight, hetero, dominant guy. Because they're actually letting loose and letting go. To me, that was so much more masculine and stronger."

WHY WOULD A GUY WANT TO TAKE ON A SUBMISSIVE ROLE IN BED?

Why would a guy want someone else to take away control from his groin?

"Their whole life they've been controlled by their dick," said Hawn. "If you control their dick and say when they can come, how they can come, how you're going to do it, it can be a relief.

"I've thought about it a lot and I realized that it's really a relief for men to make it about someone else and just put themselves at a lower level where there's not this expectation to achieve, to be better than the next guy, to be great on paper."

If men didn't want to be told what to do, take orders, and worship the female form, then professional dominatrixes would have to pack up their shingles and go home.

After all, they're watching the same movies as you and getting turned on by the same strong women who take what they want from men. I've talked to enough men who lust over female superheroes, female wrestlers, or wicked women in the movies to know that the idea of handing off power to a confident woman is scorching.

"Men are so expected to be in charge of everything, and so when we let them not be, it's super-hot. They get a vacation away from themselves," said Hawn. "That's why when the guys come to the dungeon, they're like, 'Oh, finally I can just be on the bottom end of this and you will take over.' It makes them so happy because they don't get that in their daily lives."

Why do so many dudes masturbate to MILF porn? Yes, there's the dream of the horny housewife who isn't getting enough at home and is desperate for a young guy's magic cock. But it also speaks to a desire to be dominated by an experienced woman who knows what she wants. The MILF has agency. She's not a simpering, whimpering little girl crying for her "daddy" (not that there's anything wrong with that). She's like, "Get into my bedroom, eat my pussy, fuck me like I need it, and then get out." The guy is overwhelmed by her; he does whatever she says; he's in her thrall. My experience with MILF porn is not extensive, but I've watched some, and this definitely seems to be a theme.

What people don't get about submission, whether it's male or female, is that the submissive is the object of desire. They're the ones who are objectified, made to be the center of attention.

In researching this book, I've spoken to a lot of men who emphatically agreed that it's insanely sexy to cater to the sexual whims of a powerful woman. And yet, they wouldn't describe themselves as submissive. Why should they? There's no need to put a label on desire.

In a successful power dynamic, you're both getting what you want out of a sexual encounter, no one is being selfish. If you don't care what your partner wants and he's into that sort of thing, that's not selfish either. As long as it's an agreed-upon and consensual dynamic, and revisited often to make sure that everyone remains okay with it, there's nothing that can't be explored.

"I had a boyfriend who was just all about crawling to the door, right to the pussy," said Hawn. "He was just like, 'I'm a slave at your feet and right now I'm the most important thing in the room, because I'm serving you.'"

It's a way of rethinking who's setting the pace. We think

the dominant one is in charge, but really the submissive one is the one who is creating all the energy. They're giving their energy to making you feel good.

"That's when I started to understand. I was like, oh, I see why he wants to crawl to the door and plant his face in my crotch when I come in," said Hawn. "It's because he's got a purpose. He's found his calling.

"'Yeah, I made her feel good. Ding, ding, I'm an awesome person.' Once we understand that, it's not really about them being under our foot or being submissive, or being weak. It's more like, 'Have I done something good? Have I achieved something?'"

■ ■ ■

Sexual power dynamics can take place outside of the bedroom. You can be kinky in public, but no one ever has to know it. The teasing, the flirting, the delaying can build anticipation. It's also a shared secret, an intimacy, a bond you share when you're far apart.

Say you're out for dinner with your boyfriend. You casually lean in and say, "I'm wearing that amazing lingerie I showed you."

Then he says, "Oh my god, let's get out of here."

But then you say, "I think I want dessert first. Maybe another drink."

You've got him where you want him; he's dying for you. And you haven't taken off a stitch of clothing. You're in control of when you both will leave, and whether you leave together. Maybe he gets what he wants when you get home. Maybe you kiss him goodnight and leave him fantasizing.

"You're deciding when you get to give this incredibly valuable thing, your ass or breasts, or a kiss," said Tina Horn. "You're asking them, 'What are you going to do to earn it?'"

It's important to note that just because a guy is into being submissive doesn't mean he's a great person or will be a great partner. If a guy wants to be spanked, that's great, but if you don't want to, he has to respect that too. I can't think of anything worse than having a guy want to go down on me for hours and hours if I'm not in the mood for it. He's not a hero if he's only doing it for himself.

Everyone needs to get something out of the power dynamic, otherwise there is no power dynamic.

"You are dominating from a place of equality," said Tina Horn. "Your partner is submitting from a place of equality. It wouldn't work if you weren't."

PUTTING IT ALL INTO ACTION (NO TOYS REQUIRED)

Wait, do you have a box full of expensive toys? No? No problem.

It's a total myth that you have to spend a fortune on gear to have kinky fun. You only need your words and imagination to get things moving. It's all about getting into a different headspace.

When pro-dommes meet with clients, they set a mood to help prepare for what's going to happen. After all, they're there for an experience, an escape, a fantasy. They want to be taken to another world.

"My play space is devoid of images that could be distractions. For example, there are no photos of body parts or 'sexy' pictures," said Dia Domina Dynasty. "I like to make sure there are no ambient noises or weird smells that would disturb the tranquility of the session. I tend to not change the furniture or decor around too much, so that my client can come to expect a predictably peaceful entry into the session."

It all starts in your preferred kinky space, which, for most of us, is our bedroom.

The kinky couples I spoke to for this book told me that they set dates on their calendars to make sure that they have the time to enjoy a night of filthy joy. Not everyone has the budget or space in their homes to create a kinky fuck palace, but you can still transform your bedroom (or guest room, or any room) into another world if you're creative (and have time to put it all back together before your kids or roommates come home). If there's dirty laundry and work papers all around, you're going to have problems getting into the zone.

Scents, music, all these things can set a mood that signals that you're about to enter a space and that everyone is about to assume a role. It could be a candle that you only light during kinky sessions. A perfume that you only wear during sex. There could be a certain kind of lighting, a special playlist of songs that put you into the scene. It's all about creating the setting and getting you and your partner into a specific frame of mind.

Think back to your other self. What makes you Mistress Jane? It could be a certain pair of heels, a shade of nail polish. Maybe it's a certain bra and panty set or a pair of fishnet stockings. It's whatever allows you to play out that side of yourself. Think of your power talisman, that piece of jewelry that transforms you from a woman with a day job into a goddess.

Before you begin any kinky scene, you need to take time for negotiation.

Start by talking about what sounds good, what you want to try (and what's a nonstarter), and then work within that set of constraints. Be specific about what you want to happen. Just because you're planning out what can happen, that won't ruin the spontaneity. There can (and will) still be shocks and surprises and holy shit moments.

"When I meet with a client, I ask them, what do you look for in a session? What do you enjoy? Why? How does it make you feel? But that's it. Then I like to take it from there," said

Mistress Ava Zhang. "It's not like I say 'I'm going to give you five whacks, and then I'm going to slap you three times. I'm going to spit on your nipples and then I'm going to take you to the bathroom and pee on you.' Then I'm not even looking forward to the session, because I already know what to expect."

Instead of just using this time to say what you want, use it to say *why* you want it.

"If you say, 'Honey, I'd like to handcuff you,' your partner may say, 'Um, what?' But if you say, 'Honey, it really turns me on when you don't have any control and I have all the power to do whatever I want to you,' then you're framing it like that on a more universal, emotional level."

This can give your partner time to ask important questions, like whether it's okay if you didn't handcuff him to the headboard because he's worried it will hurt his wrists. All of this can ensure that the fun will go off without a hitch and nothing will come up that could have been dealt with beforehand. Now set your safe word. You're ready to do anything you both agree to do.

Let's get back to kinky sex without toys. Mental bondage requires no gear, and it's just as erotic, if not more. Using your voice to restrain someone can be hotter than a pair of handcuffs.

"Unlike rope bondage or device bondage, mental bondage isn't physically imposed," writes Mistress Couple in *The Ultimate Guide to Bondage*.[3] "Rather, it requires that the submissive act be based upon the will of the dominant partner."

In the world of serious BDSM and kink, mental bondage can get much more elaborate, but for our purposes, it's using our words to get someone to do what we want them to do. It can mean telling your partner to keep his hands at his sides and not move them until you say so. It can mean he can't touch himself until you give him permission. It can mean ordering your partner to keep his hands against the wall or behind his back. It can mean telling him to close his eyes.

Dominating someone in the bedroom with your words is the ultimate act of power.

"I don't need to leave marks on your body," said Goddess Samantha. "I want to leave marks in your mind that nobody else will see."

Many people mistake mental bondage as a "safe" form of bondage, because there are no tools involved that could maim or physically injure someone, but that is far from the truth.

It's important to remember that words can sting more than whips and chains. Safe words are important in mental domination too. Hurt feelings will ruin a hot session faster than a flick of a poorly aimed flogger. Sex, whether it's kinky or vanilla, is all about trust and communication. If you don't have that, then you cannot safely play.

No matter what role you're taking on in the bedroom, remember you can set your own rules through the negotiation process. It's up to you both to put boundaries around what you want to do and have done to you so you ultimately get what you want.

A successful sexual power dynamic is like a scale of justice. You're giving and taking according to your desires. You're both getting what you want.

Again, consent, negotiation, and respect for boundaries are key. As long as you're both feeling good about what you're doing, then anything goes.

FEELING GOOD ABOUT IT ALL AFTERWARD

So you had a kinky scene. Nice! Now what?

This is the most important time of all, because you've just been through this wild thing together. Feelings may have come up; moments may have occurred that you want to discuss. Kink can be very, very emotional. After all, you've both revealed deep or dark parts of yourself, maybe for the first time.

After care isn't just a "You okay, babe?" It's about how you shed your roles and integrate back into your regular selves. It's how you settle back into the loving world of equal partnership. It's when you high-five each other, listen to each other, console each other, learn from each other.

"After care is essential to come down from the intense emotions that can come up from BDSM and kink," said Tina Horn. "There's something we call top space, or dom space— this rush where you're like, 'Oh my god, I'm in charge and I have the control and I'm calling the shots and it's about my pleasure right now and I'm just using you. This is fantastic.'

"That's not real life. You need a way to come down and reintegrate from that."

There's also sub space.

"It can be a blissful place where someone is saying 'I am totally surrendering and letting go and I'm here for your pleasure, however you want to use me,'" said Horn. "But after all that, it's important to hear your partner say 'You're still a human being. You're not just a hole.'"

After care is when you bring each other back to neutral or to equal. It can be jarring or feel strange. Putting comfort rituals in place can ease the transition.

"Maybe it's taking a shower so that you're not wearing that red lipstick anymore, you wash off that perfume," said Horn. "Maybe you take off your kinky clothes together, get comfortable, and split a bowl of ice cream. It's whatever makes the two of you feel reconnected afterward."

There's no one way to come down after an intense or staggering session. We all have different needs and process things differently. Say you or your partner experienced something in a scene that brought up something traumatic or scary. One of you may feel comfortable talking about it right afterward, but the other may need a day or two to let it all sink in before they can talk about it. That's okay, as long as you commit to following up afterward and making sure that you're both feeling okay.

After care is continued communication and connection. If you don't want to stick around for the after care, don't do the kink. It's as simple as that.

THIS SOUNDS GREAT, BUT WHAT IF I WANT TO BE THE SUBMISSIVE?

You're reading all of this and you're like, yes, I'm into it. I love the attitude, I love the power, but I want to be manhandled, I want to be tied up, handcuffed, humiliated. I want to tell my partner what to do, but I want him to do things to *me*.

"A woman that can communicate that she wants to be dominated and how and why she wants it is taking on a mature role," said Brame. "She's stopped being a little girl about sex, and is owning being a woman."

All the same rules apply. Say what you want, be specific; set boundaries, limits, and safe words.

"You can totally top from the bottom, of course," said Hawn. "You just have to communicate it. You can't just say 'I want you to dominate me.' You need to say how and why."

Whatever your inclination, kink, or desire, whether you want to switch it up or play a role, you have to understand that you're in control.

Congratulations! You're an adult.

YOU MUST ALLOW YOUR DESIRE TO EVOLVE

*The person who is the most sex-negative
in a relationship usually wins.*

—GLORIA BRAME

At the beginning of any relationship, two people practically need a fire extinguisher by the bed, because they're burning up the sheets. Or the car. Or the beer-soaked futon. When we're young and in love with a lot of time to spend in bed, passion seems like an infinite resource. And then, five, ten, or fifteen years later . . . *zzz*.

This wasn't supposed to happen.

Women's magazines are always telling us ways to "spice up" our relationships like they're a goulash that needs more paprika, but it takes more than a tube of edible lube and a can of whipped cream to keep two people sexually in sync after many years of being together. I used to edit a sex column back in my women's magazine days and I still cringe at some of the "tips" I helped write. Turning your hubby's La-Z-Boy into a "crazy toy" was kind of hilarious, but also absurd and probably violated the furniture's warrantee. Besides, who wants to fuck on a chair that's probably full of crumbs?

According to what I've read in *People* magazine, love has three stages: hot romance, marital bliss, and heartbreak. There are never dull moments or dishes in the sink. Does David Beckham ever pass out on the couch after watching documentaries on Netflix? Or does Jennifer Garner spend her Monday nights vacuuming up cat hair? Not according to anything I've read on line at the supermarket.

"I always joke that if Brad and Angelina can't make it work, who can?" said Hudsy Hawn. "But they're just people. Everybody gets boring, because we're creatures that want to explore. Even women, who are supposed to be nurturers and nesters, we still get antsy. We want to feel like we're still sexy."

There are so many beautiful things about being in a committed relationship. There's love, history, the knowledge of every inch of each other's skin, the comfort, the ease. All the dating bullshit finally stops, and you both can just be yourselves. You can skip going out for dinner and order in Chinese food and eat it on the couch in your sweatpants. You can cry and share your feelings about your day without worrying or caring that you're boring the other person. You can safely retreat back into yourself without feeling like you have to perform.

It's only natural for our sex lives to cool off a little. Once we commit to each other, life gets more complicated. And one thing comes after another. Planning a wedding, buying a home, deciding to have kids, dealing with illnesses and deaths . . . Our brains can only handle so much!

We fall out of sync. One person is tired one night, and then when they're in the mood, the other is tired. Then you both realize that weeks or months will have gone by without any intimacy. So you try to keep it going. Because isn't that what the magazines told us to do?

We all knew going in that marriage or long-term relationships take work. But when sex feels like work, it can start to feel like a drag.

And after several years of trying, it can become *a thing*.

It should be so easy to turn to your partner and say, "I want to open up the marriage" or "I know we've been having sex in these three positions for the last ten years, but, honey, I really want you to spank me, shove my panties in my mouth, and tell me that I'm a dirty girl."

But, um, it's not.

Even as we advance in our careers, upgrade from futons to sofas, and transform into better and more developed versions of our young selves, we are somehow shocked and ashamed when we discover that our sexualities have evolved as well.

Telling your partner that you want to radically shake up your sex life can be scarier than refinancing a mortgage or deciding to have a second kid. What if your partner is appalled? What if he laughs? What if he tells you something that you may not be ready to hear? At the same time, you may be grateful for what you have and don't want to lose it. That can make you feel guilty for wanting more. It's introducing unknown things into your good thing, something that's been stable as it is for a long time.

Sometimes, we're not even sure *what* we want, but we know it's something different. This is the time to start asking yourself some big questions.

HOW HAVE I CHANGED?

When we're young, we're still figuring out who we are. Maybe you were turned on by taking on a submissive role in bed back then. Why? Who knows? It was new. It was wild. Someone was telling you how to give pleasure, and you got pleasure from that. It felt transgressive; it turned our worlds upside down. It spoke to things that happened in our pasts, things that we weren't fully ready to process.

But just because we loved that when we were twenty-three, or with that one particular partner, doesn't mean we'll love it with all our partners. Or that it gives us the same rush it did then. Later, motherhood changes the way we experience when and how we want pleasure. Sex can be painful in the months after giving birth, especially after having a C-section or episiotomy. There's a baby latched to your nipple; there's another kid clinging to you. You're "touched out."

On the positive side, sex in our late thirties and forties can be wild. We're older; we're hotter; we care a lot less about what people think of us. Hopefully, we have a better idea of what turns us on, and don't feel compelled to do things in bed that we don't feel like doing. Our hormones may go into overdrive; we may find ourselves making cougar jokes, and have a new appreciation for the younger men in the office.

Then, perimenopause, which not enough people know or talk about, can also throw our hormones into the blender. What was wet can suddenly go dry. There are hot flashes. Our monthly periods may become biweekly tsunamis; our skin may go haywire.

All of the above are major changes to our bodies and brains. These changes are cataclysmic. And no matter how we feel about it or cope with it, it naturally affects our sex drives.

"Menopause can really change your whole state of mind about sex," said Gloria Brame. "There are very few women who come out of it feeling as sexy as they once did. But that doesn't mean you lose desire."

So why do we hold on to a singular idea of who we are as sexual beings when we are constantly undergoing so much change?

Professional dominatrixes may work with couples who find themselves in a different stage of life and struggling to figure out what to do with their changing sexual needs and wants. Many of the women I spoke to for this book host workshops to help committed couples get in touch with different sides of themselves and help them navigate new chapters in their erotic lives. They may be too nervous to talk to a sex therapist, or don't want to talk about their intimate issues with a stranger sitting across from them on a couch. Prodommes can act as a neutral party, or help couples put words to their longings.

Lucy Sweetkill works with couples who want to add excitement to their relationships. Often her goal is to help them begin to talk about how they've changed since the relationship began. This is often the hardest conversation they've ever had. Couples can share a bed for years but never feel comfortable talking about what they've been lacking.

"I work with a lot of couples who haven't ever had those conversations. They've never asked each other, what do you like? What do you enjoy?" said Sweetkill. "They get along as people, and that's great, and that can build intimacy, but they haven't actually talked about the details of how they like to be touched and what they like to hear, what activities they might like to do, what they might want to explore."

When she talks to couples about their issues, she recommends focusing on the present versus the past. Couples can experience a lot of resentment and want to talk about how they "should" be feeling versus what they're actually experiencing. Sweetkill says it's not enough to know what isn't working; couples need to come to the table with a firm idea of who they are now and what they want their sexual future to look like both as individuals and as a committed partnership.

"I always ask to speak to couples individually, because

sometimes, it's easier for them to speak freely when the other partner is not there," said Sweetkill. "It's one thing to know what your mate wants. But the question I always ask is, 'What do *you* want?'"

We weren't all raised in households that talked openly about sex. *Sex and the City* showed us that we can talk to our friends about our intimate lives, but who among us has a Samantha to make us feel comfortable revealing our fetishes, desires, and fears?

I asked my friends what their mothers told them about sex growing up, and I got quite an array of responses. Some were encouraging ("make sure that you're always having fun"), some were cautious ("always use protection"), some were totally unhelpful ("you'll learn when you get married"), and some were eye-opening and sad ("I wish I knew").

In a perfect world, we'd be able to register for a handbook on sexual communication when we get married, along with our towels and silverware. It's pretty sad that we know what sheets we want, but we can't talk about what we want to do in them after we put them on the bed.

"We grow up in cultures and with religions that tell you that you're not supposed to talk about sex in any capacity," said Sweetkill. "So then, even in our most intimate relationships, we don't know how to talk about any kind of intimacy, let alone physical intimacy."

We can read all the relationship books and articles we want, but there's never going to be a one-size-fits-all answer. Every couple—and more importantly, every person—brings a different perspective into the equation.

"I had a couple come into the dungeon and this guy said, 'I want her to dominate me, but I don't think she can do it, because of this and that,'" said Hudsy Hawn. "And she's sitting there all quiet and I thought, *Well, look at what you're doing.*

You're shooting her down, and yeah, you're right. You just told her she can't do it. And if you want to be the submissive, you need to be quiet and let her do the talking."

What we don't know about our partners can fill volumes. It's crazy to think that just because you've known someone for years and years, that you know what's on their minds and what they're capable of.

Telling a person you've shared your life with for years that you want something radically different takes guts. For some people, it's easier to keep those desires a secret than to share them with the person they love for fear of rejection.

It takes emotional work to fix a relationship that's been silenced on the erotic front. You could both order all the sex toys in the catalog but all the dildos in the world aren't going to fix a relationship that's broken on the communication front.

Committed couples may still be having sex where both partners experience orgasms, yet still feel unsatisfied. That can be really confusing. Aren't orgasms the point? Shouldn't that be enough?

HOW TO BEGIN THE TALK

Be strategic about where and when to have these conversations. For example, ironically, bed may actually not be the best place to start.

"You want to talk in a place where you both feel like you're on an equal playing field," said Sweetkill. "Your bedroom is not an equal playing field. After sex is not a good time to bring these things up. You're literally naked, you're at your most vulnerable. Be willing to just sit down and have that conversation outside of a heated or intense moment."

The *way* we ask questions is just as important as what questions we ask.

"It's best to ask questions and make statements that avoid blame and judgment," said Sweetkill. "Yes, own your feelings. But 'You make me feel this way' can sound a lot more accusing than 'I feel like I want to explore this' or 'I feel that there are things that maybe I'm missing.' This can be more effective than a conversation that starts with 'I hate it when you' or 'Why don't you ever . . .'"

Think about how you'd like to be approached, and how you'd like someone to consider your feelings. You're not just telling your partner that you need things to change. You're saying that your partnership is worth preserving and that you'd like to evolve together.

"Tell your partner that they're in a safe space to talk," she said. "And there's no judgment. Let it be really clear that you want this to be a thoughtful conversation. And that you're really listening."

You can ask questions without making it feel like an interrogation. But know that your partner may not be used to these kinds of questions; they may feel put on the spot or shy, or just draw a blank. Your partner probably hasn't been thinking about things the same way you have. You may be taking them by surprise. Ask specific questions that help them give you more useful answers. And be patient!

We all want relationships where we can express ourselves without fear of rejection. Asking "Why are you into that?" isn't as helpful as "Can you tell me more about that?"

The whole point is to soften feelings of judgment and shame for both of you. No one wants to feel shut down or like they were wrong to be vulnerable.

If you want to try something different in bed, try painting a picture of all the ways it would turn you on, and how it might turn your partner on too. Use adjectives; bring in the senses; create a scenario. Share the song you hear in your head when you're both doing that naughty thing. Compare it to a scene in a movie you watched together. Instead of just blurting it out, use your imagination to show your partner that this is something you want to experience together, to increase your connection and bring you closer.

Remember our old friend, *Fifty Shades of Grey*? Having something concrete to point to can be a great way to start talking about the things that have been on your mind. You can mention an article you read about bondage or power dynamics and ask your partner what they think.

"It's a good way of testing out what they feel about something," said Sweetkill. "You can get a sense of how the conversation will go and hopefully, you can begin to dig deeper together. "Filling in the details and color can help your partner understand where you're coming from. I find that just doing that work alone makes a couple a lot more comfortable with exploring."

Consider taking an afternoon to put your thoughts on paper. Dedicating time to this task can bring more things to mind and allow your thoughts to breathe. You can anticipate things that may come up and have ideas about how to address them with more confidence.

Okay, you've scheduled time to talk. You're both sitting at the kitchen table and enjoying a glass of wine. Worried that when the time comes you'll be tongue-tied? Try reading from your notes. Ask that your partner not say anything until you're finished. Say what you need to say using openhearted, nonjudgmental language, and then open up the floor to questions. Laughing and blushing are okay, and encouraged. Just get it out there, and congratulate yourself for starting this brave and necessary conversation.

Just know that you may not get the answer you want—at least not in the moment. For example, if you want to open up the relationship or try out acting as a different gender, or you're questioning your sexual orientation, prepare yourself for pushback—or shock, or tears.

Expect that changing the course of your sexual future is going to take more than one conversation. The first one may not go the way you want but you've already taken the hardest step.

You've said "I want."

MAYBE IT'S NOT JUST ABOUT THE SEX

Ideally, the two of you will have more great conversations, take some leaps, figure out what you both like and can live with. *Woot!* A whole new world of wild adventure awaits you both.

But this scenario assumes that all that was missing from your sexual lives was communication and honesty. It assumes that the rest of your relationship was in good shape on all the other fronts.

This is where things get gnarly. Not everyone is blessed with the same level of communication skills. Some weren't raised to think that way; others aren't socialized to access or express their feelings. It's totally normal for your partner to need time to process things. After all, not everyone has a prepared answer to "What do you think about tying me up?"

If your "Here's what I want to try" conversation breaks down or goes off the rails, the larger question may not be "Can we communicate about this?" but "Are we able to communicate at all?"

If you've been struggling to communicate about other aspects of your relationship, it's going to be even harder to get clarity about what's bothering you in the bedroom. Talking about sex, whether it's kinky or vanilla, is just hard. Again, if only there was a handbook to teach committed couples how to talk about intimacy and a mandate that you both read it and update it yearly.

No one is born knowing how to talk about sex and desire.

"These types of communication skills don't just come naturally," said Sweetkill. "I think most people end up learning them by going to therapy or doing their own self-exploration and research. No one is born with it."

It could be time to think about how the two of you communicate about things in general. Do you often find yourselves at an impasse? Do you find that the two of you often leave discussions, even ones that have nothing to do with your relationship, feeling annoyed or frustrated? Because if you do, adding sex to the mix may be adding a huge strain to something that's already vulnerable. It's easy for a talk about sex to turn ugly and accusatory. It can reveal your disappointments about other aspects of the relationship.

It can be shattering to reveal your heart and deepest desires and have them rejected or dismissed.

"One of the most profound observations I've had as a sex therapist is that the person who is the most sex-negative in a relationship usually wins," said Brame.

There may not be a *Fifty Shades of Grey* ending for the two of you.

"If you keep trying things with a partner, and they keep pushing back, I guarantee you BDSM, kink, or sex is not the only problem," said Sweetkill. "Ask yourself, is this one problem, or is this one of a bunch of problems?"

Each of the professional dominatrixes I spoke to all said the same thing. You can try to add kink into your relationship, but there's no guarantee that it will be the answer to what's ailing it. It's easy to make changes to a house when there are only a few bricks on the foundation, but it's a lot harder to when the whole house has already been built.

You may just have to face the fact that you've grown in different sexual directions and that it's impossible to make your sex lives mesh in a way that you both find satisfying.

"Unfortunately, this happens with a lot of couples. They came into it a long time ago, one person is one way, one person's another way," said Sweetkill. "And the hard truth about when one person is becoming more self-aware and the other person isn't, is that that relationship may not work anymore."

If you ultimately decide that your kinks or your sexual happiness isn't just a "nice to have" but a "need to have," then you've got some tough decisions ahead of you.

"I've seen clients do a lot of self-work by going to therapy, by seeing a dominatrix and exploring their own sexuality and having these deeper conversations with themselves and with others," said Sweetkill. "Then, after trying many ways to try to share what they've learned about themselves to the person they love, they realize their partner is just closed off to it all."

It's terrifying to walk away from something that you've had and built and maintained for ten, fifteen, twenty years. The guilt, the shame, the fear of the unknown. It's unfathomable.

And if you have children, a mortgage, or a life that you love, this question is especially hard to answer. No empathetic pro-domme, sex therapist, or kink writer can tell you what to do, or whether you'll end up happier than where you started.

That's the good and bad part of exploring. The good is finding out who you really are and how you've changed. The bad is that you may not get what you want. But it doesn't mean it's not worth pursuing! If anything, it makes it more important.

"I mean, it sounds very obvious, but you can't take a jerk

person and mold him into your sexual fantasy, because he'd be still kind of a jerk," said Brame. "You could work together to try to realize each other's fantasies. But you also have to be real with who you're with."

Back to the tired metaphor of "spice." Kink can add some "spice" to a relationship, but a relationship is not a recipe. Couples that are into kink, whether it's 24/7, once a week, or whenever the kids are staying with Grandma, love it because they're finally able to express their deepest, freakiest, personal selves. It's a relief; it's exhilarating; it's pure fun and joy. It's a way for them to express their adoration for each other. It's seeing and being seen. That's what makes it magical.

Kinky language can help us put our relationships into focus because it demands that we keep questioning, digging, asking, wanting, and evolving. It's a framework to examine your life and whether you feel like you're in a power dynamic that's working for you. It's natural for the balances to shift over time. But consent, negotiation, and trust can also keep us honest with each other. If we can't feel safe telling the other our deepest feelings, then things may have drifted far off course.

If you want your partner to be more submissive or more dominant (or want to change any aspect of your sexual lives) you need to look—realistically—at the content of their character first. You have to know who they are and what they're capable of giving.

"I have to say, I have never known a partner who truly, genuinely loved their wife or husband who wouldn't make an effort to please them," said Brame. "Sex is teamwork. That means fifty-fifty effort."

QUIZ:
AM I SECRETLY KINKY?

Let's get out our #2 pencils or blue ink ballpoint pens. You have my permission to fill out your answers on the page, because if I remember correctly, there's nothing naughtier than writing in your textbooks.

(Note: Do *not* do this if it's a library book. The only thing more terrifying than an angry dominatrix is a pissed-off librarian.)

1. Darling, it's just you and me tonight. Let's:

a. See if some friends want to come over for dinner and drinks.

b. Have some alone time, wink wink, nudge nudge.

c. Break out the toys and get freaky.

d. See if some friends want to come over and get out the webcam.

2. Have you ever had a sexual fantasy about a teacher?

    a. Nah.

    b. Maybe that one cute Spanish teacher.

    c. Don't get me started on Mr./Ms. Jones! I still think about him/her.

    d. Yes, do you know anyone who can give me detention? I've been terribly remiss in my studies.

3. Masturbation is:

    a. Something I'm really shy about.

    b. Sex with someone I love.

    c. Best when we're doing it together.

    d. Best when you're doing it when I tell you to.

4. My last lover was really kinky! One time, we:

    a. Did it while his parents were in the next room.

    b. Did it in the bathroom of a dive bar.

    c. Went to a sex party.

    d. Last lover?

5. Don't look in my underwear drawer! That's where I keep my:

    a. Um, underwear?

    b. Vibrator.

    c. Vibrator plus a few other, *ahem*, things.

d. Vibrator(s), sex toys, rope, restraints, ball gags . . . wait, that's two drawers.

6. Do you ever fantasize about having a threesome?

a. Nope.

b. It's fun to think about it, but I don't think I could actually go through with it.

c. I'm swiping through a threesome app on my phone right now.

d. Alice is already coming over with Joe and Tina. Don't you mean a six-some?

7. Quick, here's a cucumber: What's the first thing that comes to mind?

a. A salad?

b. Don't make me say it.

c. A big ol' dick.

d. Aw, my King Cock Girthy Ultra Realistic Suction Cup Dildo. Memories . . .

8. Who was the first person you ever had a sexual fantasy about?

a. One of the boys in the neighborhood.

b. One of the guys in a boy band.

c. Whoever my parents thought was a bad influence.

d. Jesus Christ.

9. When I watch sporting events, I find myself wishing:

a. That I did not have to watch sporting events.

b. I could see what some of the players looked like naked.

c. That they would all get me alone in the locker room and . . . wait, what was the question?

d. That I was the ball.

10. I'm a professional dominatrix. In three words, what do I do?

a. I don't know.

b. Beat up dudes.

c. Play with power.

d. Explore human connection.

11. May I spank you?

a. Please don't.

b. Okay, but be gentle.

c. I've always got a hankerin' for a spankerin'.

d. Yes please, and will you use the split tail whip this time? Although I do love that wooden paddle you got me for my birthday . . .

12. Will you spank me?

a. Under no circumstances.

b. I guess I could if you want me to.

c. Get yer butt over here.

d. Yes, we negotiated this. Assume the position.

13. Have you ever had a sexual fantasy about a cartoon character?

a. What is actually wrong with you?

b. Ha, no.

c. Maybe I had a thing for She-Ra. And one of the My Little Ponies.

d. Funny you should ask; My Aladdin costume is about to come out of the dryer.

14. Would you ever act out one of your dark fantasies?

a. I suppress all my dark fantasies.

b. Yikes, it would have to be with a very special person.

c. I've already acted out one or two.

d. I've booked my weekend at La Domaine Esemar and I'm counting the days.

15. Wanna look at some porn?

a. No, it's gross and degrading.

b. Only if I know that everyone involved is there of their own free will.

c. Yes, omg, have you seen what Lust Cinema is doing? HOT!

d. Sure, I'm about to shoot a video this weekend, wanna come along?

16. Congrats, you just received a free copy of *Bow Down*! What are you gonna do with it?

    a. Immediately regift it.

    b. Read it in bed tonight.

    c. Put it out on my coffee table.

    d. Turn to the page where Lindsay quoted me as an expert! She'd better have spelled my name right!

17. I want to go down on you for hours and hours. I expect nothing in return. How does that make you feel?

    a. I'm calling the police.

    b. What's the catch?

    c. If you're okay with not getting off tonight, it sounds fucking awesome.

    d. That all is right with the world.

18. Honey, I want you to dominate me in the bedroom. What do you think?

    a. I don't know what that means, but I'm pretty sure I'll hate it.

    b. I would if I knew how.

    c. Interesting! Tell me everything you've been fantasizing about.

    d. Yes, the bedroom. And every room. And all rooms.

19. **How do you feel about bodily fluids?**

    a. What about them?

    b. Not in the face. Wait, what?

    c. You can pee on me, but I can't promise I won't laugh.

    d. Which ones? I'm only asking because my washing machine is broken.

20. **What my partner and I get up to in the privacy of our home is:**

    a. Giving me anxiety just thinking about it.

    b. Nobody's business.

    c. Nobody's business except for a few special friends; they know who they are.

    d. Nobody's business except for my friends, subscribers, subs, fellow fetishists . . .

21. **Do you think that both partners need to have an orgasm to experience great sex?**

    a. I would like to experience an orgasm, period.

    b. I mean, yeah, ideally both people get off.

    c. We can trade off. One time it's about me; the next it's about my partner.

    d. An orgasm is nice, but a full mind-body connection is the greater goal.

22. How important is penetration during sex?

a. How else can you have sex?

b. It's fun, but there's other stuff to do.

c. It's great as long as you know you don't need an actual dick to do it.

d. Why limit yourself?

23. Will you peg me?

a. Is that a Pinterest thing?

b. Oh man.

c. If you think you'd like it, I'm willing to try it.

d. Anytime, my darling.

24. Can a man experiment with taking on a more submissive role in bed and still be considered "masculine"?

a. I'd really struggle with that.

b. I think so, but can he dominate me sometimes?

c. I think that sounds pretty cool.

d. This whole question blows my mind. Is it the 1950s?

25. Have you ever been friends with a sex worker?

a. No.

b. I think my friend from college worked as a dominatrix for a while.

c. Sure, I know lots of cool people.

d. I count them among my best friends.

26. Can you imagine pain being pleasurable?

a. No, I cannot imagine that it ever could.

b. Maybe a lil spankin'.

c. Definitely.

d. They are just different aspects of the same thing.

27. The idea of taking control in the bedroom is scary because:

a. That's not how I was raised to think about female sexuality.

b. I wouldn't know what to do.

c. What if I liked it so much that it changed my life and things would never be the same again?

d. I'm not sure that the hook in the ceiling can support my sex swing. That's why I keep it in the living room.

28. What's your secret dominatrix name?

a. My what now?

b. (Blush) I'm gonna have to think.

c. I've got a Mistress Vengeance inside me somewhere.

d. I'm on page 53 of this book!

29. My ideal lover has an enormous:

    a. House in Connecticut.

    b. WANG! Just kidding.

    c. Collection of sex toys and knows how to use them.

    d. Capacity for empathy.

30. I've decided to enter into a polyamorous relationship. What do you think?

    a. Are you asking me for a cracker?

    b. Whoa, that sounds . . . complicated.

    c. Nice!

    d. That you should definitely come to this party I'm throwing this weekend.

31. I want you to control my orgasm. Will you do it?

    a. Is this a Hogwarts thing?

    b. I wouldn't know how.

    c. Wow, you must trust me a lot.

    d. I will consider allowing you to come in two days, but only if you're very, very good.

32. Will you wear a collar around your neck to signal that you are mine?

    a. Fuck off.

    b. That's a little out there for me.

c. Okay, but only in the house.

d. Of course, which one shall I wear today?

33. I want to wear a collar around my neck to signify that I'm yours. What do you think?

a. Please don't.

b. That's weirdly sweet that you want to, but it's not necessary.

c. That you must be really devoted to me. I'll do my best to keep earning that privilege.

d. I've always loved you in leather with silver spikes.

34. I fantasize about a full-time, 24/7 Master or Mistress/slave relationship. How do you feel about that?

a. Disgusted.

b. Confused.

c. Intrigued.

d. Honored.

35. The scariest thing about admitting that you may be into kink is:

a. That I'd feel abnormal, or like a freak.

b. My relationship with my partner would change and we wouldn't be compatible anymore.

c. What if one kink leads to another, then another, and another, and it goes to a dark place?

d. That I waited this long to find out.

Mostly As: Blue Valentine. You're pretty freaked out by the whole idea of kink, and maybe sex and intimacy in general. And while kink isn't for everyone, it's important to figure out your own desires and not be scared of what they look like. You also may have been raised with some pretty stiff views on sex and sexuality and gender roles. I'm worried that you feel anxious in bed, and maybe, out there in the world. It's worth thinking about why certain aspects of sexual exploration terrify you so much. If you bought this book, chances are you're seeking ways to feel more powerful. That's a great step! Don't worry about being kinky; that's not where you're at right now. Just start by telling yourself that you deserve pleasure, joy, and love.

Mostly Bs: Eyes Wide Shut. I see some chocolate and rainbow sprinkles on that vanilla! You're a little shy (who isn't?), but you know there's a whole other side of sex out there that could be fun to explore if you had the courage and the right partner. You're a sex-positive person, curious, and open-minded, which is wonderful. If you want to, you can take some baby steps toward adding kink into your life. Consider checking out a workshop at your local sex shop, or ordering some of the books I recommend in the back of this book. Think about all the sexy movie scenes, dirty parts of books, and experiences you've had, and write it all down in a private journal. And then start thinking about being more confident and open-minded about what you want in bed, and let it work its way out of the sheets and into the streets. Start saying "I want" and then keep on saying it.

Mostly Cs: Tie Me Up! Tie Me Down! You've got your kinky boots on and you are kicking down all the doors. You're a sex-loving, power-playing, toy-juggling, super-communicator. And while you're not necessarily interested in trying out every kink in the book (who has the time, really), you have an adventurous spirit, and you're down and totally eager to try most things. But most importantly, you understand that the purpose of sex is pleasure and joy, not just the mechanics of bangin' parts. You're not afraid to venture into unchartered waters (or watersports), and you are comfortable taking the lead in the bedroom as well as taking the time to listen to the needs and desires of others. Godspeed, you kinkster. Keep exploring!

Mostly Ds: The X-Files. You are playing at sex, sensuality, power, and empathy at the highest level. You are at home with yourself and your kinks and you're not afraid to dive into your deepest depths. Kink isn't just something you do; it's who you are, it's in every fiber of your being. You talk it, walk it, work it, and it drives your relationships with other people and to the world at large. The language of power dynamics is your second language, and getting off in ways that would horrify the religious right has always been what you've wanted and who you are. You give no fucks about society's expectations about gender and power and what regular people think of the way you live your life. You never forget to ask people their pronouns. You're often angry at the world for being so close-minded and unjust. You are constantly rethinking and assessing who you are and how you're evolving. You play outside the rules, you conform to no category, you radiate power, you wear your kinks like Scout badges. Are you a little intimidating? Probably, but that's the world's problem, not yours.

THE POWER OF THE
SPIRIT

LESSON #12

YOU SHALL LIVE BY A CODE

Power is being able to say "You don't meet my
standards. You're not good enough for me."

—MISTRESS AVA ZHANG

It's my first day at a new job, and HR has given me a huge
packet of forms to sign. I leaf through my payroll information, my tax forms, and then I see it: the Code of Conduct.
Each company has rules, guidelines, and an ethos that I'm expected to abide by; otherwise, I may be terminated.

It may include the following:

- Always present the company's products in a manner
  consistent with its core values.

- Avoid engaging in any activity that involves the appearance of impropriety.

- Never file a report that is intended to threaten or dam-
  age an employee's reputation.

- The safety and well-being of our team members is our
  mission.

- You must abide by our safety standards.

- We do not tolerate sexual harassment or retaliation of any kind.

Companies spend a lot of money on lawyers, consultants, and branding experts to craft their Codes of Conduct. They're put in place to create their carefully crafted image for their stockholders, management, and potential employees. I sign them and hope that if I work for them, I'll be protected against unforeseen events and bad actors.

But what happens when a boss discriminates against me, or I see coworkers violate rules without ever getting in trouble with management, or watch a colleague quit in disgust after realizing that the "Code of Conduct" is really meant to protect the company and not its workers? What a waste of paper. What a waste of time.

We've all seen it: The rules apply to some and not others. Companies start off with the best intentions, and then when they expand, the principles go out the window. When companies don't abide by their own Codes of Conduct, employees become confused, and then they lose faith and trust, worse.

Yet job after job, we sign them—because they're mandatory, and, well, we need the job.

But it offers food for thought. If fast-food chains, banks, and chemical manufacturers have Codes of Conduct, why don't we as women have Codes of Conduct for what we expect of others?

Professional dominatrixes insist on enforcing their own Codes of Conduct. Their clients are mostly men who seek services that are sexual in nature. They may have dreamed for years of meeting a beautiful woman to dominate them or help them explore a complex fantasy. And many are eager to abide by the rules; a few are not. You'd think they'd be willing to follow simple instructions if they're ready to pay hundreds of dollars to have a woman discipline them.

But they're men. If you give them an inch, they'll take a mile. And if a pro-domme is in a room with a client, no matter how effectively she's screened him, interviewed him, and checked his references, she's still alone in a room with him. Her time, her body, her energy are all at risk.

We as women, nonbinary, people of color, and LGTBQ people can learn a lot from the faceless corporations who spend millions to craft these documents with the express intention of protecting themselves.

What do you expect of others? And what do you do when people violate your standards? What's your personal code of conduct?

"YOU DON'T MEET MY STANDARDS"

On Mistress Ava Zhang's[1] website's home page, rather than the more typical glamour photo in stiletto heels and shiny black latex, she's shown staring thoughtfully out of a window, glasses on, wearing a white collared shirt with a chic black leather harness crisscrossing her torso. She has a blog called *The Mind of the Mistress*, where she writes about her thoughts on dominance and submission, as well as her thoughts on women and power.

On a warm spring morning, she met me in the lobby of her luxury Manhattan apartment building. She was dressed for a relaxing Sunday in, wearing a brightly colored, loose-fitting summer dress and comfy sandals. When I went to shake her hand, she opened her arms to me for a hug instead.

Her apartment was both airy and cozy, situated toward the back of the building. "It's perfect," she said cheerfully. "No one can hear my boyfriend screaming when we have sex."

After fixing us a cup of coffee, and making sure I was comfortably set up with my laptop and recorder at her kitchen table, we sat down to talk.

"I've always been fascinated by sexuality. This fascination predates my arrival to the States, to when I was a child in China," she said. "Throughout high school and college I took every opportunity to write about sex whenever a paper was assigned."

After college, out of curiosity and "probably a bit of rebellion towards my parents," she found herself working at Dr. Susan Block's sex therapy institute and radio show in downtown Los Angeles. Every week writers, professors, porn stars, artists, and comedians shuffled in and out of there to be guests on Dr. Block's show. Zhang and others lived there. According to Zhang, Dr. Block wasn't your average sex therapist. In addition to in-person counseling, there was a phone sex therapy line. Zhang, as part of her job, manned the line and helped Block produce her radio show. But more important, she was able to learn from a woman who lived by her own rules, according to her sense of humor, style, and principles.

"I think that's what I really needed at that time in my life," she said. "I wanted to know who I was, and what it was that I really wanted in life, whether from friendship, or partners, or romance."

At twenty-six, she came back to New York and took an office job at a sex tech company. But she quickly realized that the nine-to-five life wasn't for her. Sex intrigued her; desk life, even if her job was sex-related, did not. She began to fully explore her own identity and the kind of work she wanted to be doing—and what she expected of others. After some deep introspection, a writer friend suggested that she reach out to a woman who could be a mentor. She got in touch with an

Asian-American dominatrix based in Santa Monica, and was soon on a plane to meet her.

"To be an Asian dominatrix is kind of like a fetish within a fetish," she said. "I wanted to find out some of the things I should expect and what to be cautious of when working with clients in a session. She told me to try everything. Figure out what I like. She told me that what I like will be what my clients will like. She told me that the most important thing was for me to have a lot of fun and to be happy."

Her mentor's words inspired her not only to become a professional dominatrix, but to carve out her own her personal ethos that could lay the foundations of her life and work.

"I think it's really important for every professional dominatrix to have a philosophy through which they filter their clients and their actions. A code, if you will, because if you don't, you can really fall off the tracks, especially with the promise of a lot of money," she said.

Zhang takes words very seriously. Clients who seek out her services don't just book an appointment like they would for a haircut or dental checkup. They must email her, not just asking to be seen but also to explain why they want to meet her. A thoughtful, well-written email reveals more than what the client is seeking to explore.

"I have a very strict vetting process," she said. "If a client wants to see me for the first time, they do not text me. I do not have any social media, so they can't contact me there. The only way they can get in touch with me is through an introductory email."

For Zhang, these initial communications reveal who these potential clients are as humans, and whether they are worth getting to know. Only a handful meet her standard. If the letter of introduction feels too transactional, she will likely choose not to meet with them.

A well-composed letter that reveals curiosity, introspection, and respect will make it to the next stage of the vetting process, which is a personal response from her, and then, if the communication continues to satisfy her, a phone call. This isn't just a formality. It's also part of what makes her work fulfilling.

"I feel really good about reading a beautiful letter from someone who's sincere, and really wants to see me for the right reason," she said. "Then again, I feel just as good about looking at an email from a potential client and saying, 'I don't want to see that person, so no, I'm not going to.'

"That said, the letters that do meet my standards are some of the most beautiful pieces of writing I've ever read in my entire life," she said. "It's like being wooed."

This is Mistress Ava Zhang's philosophy and code of conduct. If you do not impress her at every stage of her vetting process, there's no other way to engage her professional services.

A person who intrigues her and is deemed worthy of her time will get the benefit of her skills, her years of experience, and access to her personhood. That person should feel honored.

To her, being able to say no to someone who doesn't meet her criteria is powerful.

"Power is saying 'I don't need that right now. No thank you. This is not meeting my standards,'" she said. "You're not good enough for me. It's all about how to refuse, and how to leave any situation, relationship, client, whatever it is. That's your power. That's your confidence."

YOU WILL DEMAND MORE

Why do we congratulate terrible people for doing the bare minimum? Think about how many times a day we say the words "at least."

"At least he listens to me when I have a bad day."

"At least he texts me back."

"At least he remembered my birthday."

"At least my boss isn't a total asshole."

"At least he pays child support."

"At least he doesn't hit me."

"At least I'm not alone."

"By saying 'at least,' we're guarding our hearts against terror, loneliness, and failure," said Dawn Serra. "When we say 'at least,' we're comforting ourselves, but we're also settling for a fraction of our deserved happiness."

Realizing that you've been settling for less can be an epiphany, but it can also be terrifying. Whether it's leaving a bad relationship, moving to a new city, or starting your own business. It takes a lot of faith to demand more—from yourself and from others.

To Zhang, power means being able to demand what you're worth and then walk away if you don't get it. That can take years of building up your skills, your relationships, your inner resources, and making your financial security a priority.

We all have to pay rent; it isn't always easy to turn down a paycheck when bills are due. But it's essential to our happiness to create and maintain a high standard for our partners and friends. Who gets to be near you? What do they bring to the table? Are they helping you live the life that you're striving to lead, or are they wasting your time and draining your confidence?

"I think something that transcends culture and language is the intention of the person. Do they want to bring joy to your life or respect in your presence? Every culture has a way of doing this," said Zhang. "When I'm talking to somebody, do they say, 'It was nice meeting you,' in whatever way they do it? Do they shake hands? Do they see me to the door? Do they open the door? I'm a little bit old-fashioned in certain ways, I have to admit.

"When we do meet, are they going to be on time? Are they going to let me know if they're going to be running late ahead of time? If they did end up being late and causing me to wait, do they offer to pay?"

Our Codes of Conduct give us the power to say no to people that disappoint us. They give us the power to ask more from relationships and from ourselves. It gives us a standard to live up to.

"I'm surrounded by super-perverted and awesome friends, and I've met really great clients who I would be friends with outside of a session," she said. "I have a partner who is super submissive to me, and allows me to be who I am with him or other people that I play with."

After the interview was over, she rode the elevator down to the lobby with me, and then walked me out into the street. She gave me another warm hug, made sure I knew how to get home, and waved goodbye.

Later, I'd think back to how generous she'd been and how she constantly checked in with me to make sure that I was comfortable in her home. She took her time answering questions and weighed her answers carefully. When she didn't want to address a topic, she said so in a kind, honest, and direct manner. When she walked me down to the lobby, I felt like a treasured person, someone who deserved to be seen to the door.

There had been so many power moves but none of them had been aggressive or controlling. She was simply holding herself to the standard that she expects of others.

"My code is kindness, consent, and graciousness," she said. "If those things are present in a person, then we can talk about what kind of perverted fun we can get into."

Since interviewing Mistress Zhang, I've created my own Code of Conduct. I wrote it over the course of the months writing this book. It wasn't an easy process. I had to look back at times when my standards hadn't been high enough, when I'd allowed unworthy people access to my heart. I had to ask myself why I had been so thoughtless with myself and why I'd felt I'd deserved so little. This list went beyond personal relationships, family, and friendships. It got me thinking of all the times I'd suffered in silence, sulked, or just accepted what I thought I couldn't change. I had lived so much of my life defensively, taking things as they came. I never said "I want." I ignored the things I needed. I hadn't thought of myself as worthy of having a standard at all.

I wrote this book because I wanted all that to change.

Here's my Code of Conduct. I'm trying every day to live up to it.

All of my relationships must bring me joy.

I will not attempt to read anyone's mind.

I will not expect anyone to read my mind.

I will be kind, honest, and direct in all my communications.

I will not be passive aggressive; I will tackle things head-on.

I deserve to take time for myself when I need it.

My interests, especially the weird ones, are worth exploring.

I will not lie to myself.

My body and mind deserve care and protection.

I will be a good listener and keep empathy in my heart.

I will walk away from people who don't show me the same respect I've given them.

My dreams are worth pursuing.

I can sit with my thoughts. I do not have to decide now.

My Code of Conduct is setting a template for the kind of life I want to live and for the person I want to be. It reflects my values, beliefs, and philosophy. It's taking my life back into my hands and showing me a way forward.

It's my own personal power.

YOU ARE ALWAYS A WORK IN PROGRESS

I determine my own worth.

—DIA DOMINA DYNASTY

It isn't easy being a queen in a world full of unworthy subjects. Professional dominatrixes know better than anyone that in order to get through all the tough stuff that life throws us, we have to have thick skins, to be adaptable, but always to hold on to who we are and what we ultimately want.

Personal power evolves over time. We rise up; we get pushed back. We learn from it. We keep moving. We are resilient. But man, it's hard to feel like a Mistress when we spend so much of our lives feeling angry, depressed, helpless, and, well, powerless.

Nobody wants to keep "fighting the good fight" for acceptance, love, and respect. It gets us down. Our power reserves get depleted, and it can feel easier to just lie down and give in to how society expects us to look, act, be, and feel. It's so frustrating, when we're trying to be better, more honest, and more authentic, to be surrounded by linear-thinking assholes who don't bother questioning their motivations or think twice about exploiting others.

During my research for this book, the women I spoke to were brutally honest about all the ways they grapple with their identities, the law, their partners, the judgment of others, and their relationships with their bodies. They told me about the work it's taken to get to where they are and how they still grapple with self-love and acceptance. They are more powerful than they were before but getting there hasn't been easy.

WE MUST MAKE PEACE WITH OUR BODIES

Goddess Genesis is the co-owner of Sanctuary LAX, a dungeon and play space in Los Angeles. She and her wife, Mistress Cyan, run the business together and, twice a year, they organize DomCon, the convention for professional dominatrixes and other BDSM-loving kinksters that I attended while I was researching this book. DomCons are complicated multiday events, done with a small staff. There are workshops to be organized, blocks of hotel rooms to be reserved at a discounted rate, buses to arrange to transport party-ready dominatrixes to the Friday and Saturday night Fetish Balls, a Gala VIP dinner, and an awards show and mixers. There are strong personalities to manage, gift bags to distribute, vendors to satisfy, and dozens of volunteers to wrangle to make each DomCon go off without any, well, kinks.

When Goddess Genesis opened the door to her grand hotel suite to greet me, I had the feeling that I'd known her all my life. We both had brown hair, big laughs, and a gallows sense of humor. She promised to give me a real interview after the awards dinner, which was giving her anxiety. Hey, you try organizing a red-carpet event with over a hundred Alpha women, many of whom are celebrities in their own right.

True to her word, after the dust settled, we regrouped the next day, sat down, and began to chat like old friends. For Goddess Genesis, the struggle to feel at home in the world and in her body is always in the forefront of her mind.

"I was not one that did well in school, and so I thought I was never going to go to college. My dad, who was an educator, said, 'You are not dumb. Just because you didn't get good grades does not mean you can't handle college.' So I went to college and I did well, but I didn't know what the fuck I wanted to do," she said.

"Here I was at community college going on my fourth year and my dad's like, 'Look, you don't even have an associate's degree and you should have gone to a university by now. What are you doing?' I was like, 'I don't know. I want to do a lot of things and yet I'm stuck because what do I choose?' He's like, 'Get a job.'"

Genesis, like nearly all the professional dominatrixes I spoke with, told me that the path to her calling was a long and winding one. She worked as a temp, on assembly lines, learned how to do sales cold calls. She felt lost, unable to focus on any one thing. She suffered from crippling anxiety and depression through her twenties and thirties before finding her heart's work in kink.

"I've had eating disorders, I've lost and gained weight," she said. "It all started when I was eleven or twelve, I think. The sadness."

We talked for over two hours about how puberty had harpooned our self-images and sent us into a tailspin. Just as we began to bloom, we started to shrink into ourselves.

"We lock our perceptions of our bodies from when we were twelve or thirteen years old. We can stay locked into those ideas well into our twenties, thirties, and beyond. That was definitely true for me," she said.

These terrible feelings, they seep into our adulthood, warping our views of what our bodies are capable of and the treatment they deserve, from ourselves and others. It's tough to see ourselves as we really are now versus how we felt when we were young and powerless.

"I went through years of depression and suicidal feelings through high school and college," she said. "When I was twenty-four, I took everything that was in the medicine cabinet—Tylenol, aspirin, allergy pills, oh, and of course diet pills.

"It's pretty comical, because was I still going to be worried about my body in death? Probably," she laughed. "I'd be like, 'Is my skeleton skinny enough?'"

When she moved to Los Angeles, she began to work in a dungeon. Like many professional dominatrixes who come up through a house of domination, she began as a professional submissive before training to become a domme. It was then that she began to grow into herself. She wanted a new start. She became Genesis, her new beginning.

Genesis told me that helping the women she works with deal with their own body issues helps to heal her own.

"Now I know that clients see me for what I can do, for my skills, and because they trust me. It's not all about my body. But in the beginning, I didn't feel that," she said. "Now I meet younger dommes who struggle with their bodies, who worry whether they're pretty enough. Being their cheerleader helps me to feel better about my own past and what I've struggled with."

"I tell them what I tell myself, 'You have skills, and people are going to see you because of what you do, not for what you look like in latex.' You have to deal with yourself in the here and now. I used to joke that I had zero self-esteem and now I have low-esteem!" She laughs. "So yeah, that's an improvement."

■ ■ ■

Mistress Velvet is a Chicago-based pro-domme and sex educator with a graduate degree in gender studies. During her
work, she meets clients who are genuinely interested in learning more about oppression, and want to show her respect.
She may assign them texts to read and demand a one-page
essay on passages from *Sister Outsiders* by Audre Lorde, *The
New Jim Crow* by Michelle Alexander, or *The Color of Kink*
by Ariane Cruz.

Many pro-dominatrixes demand "tributes" from their clients, monetary gifts to prove their worship. Mistress Velvet
prefers to call them reparations.

"The people that come in respect me, but that's because
they aren't used to being in contact with people of color," she
told me in a phone interview. "Many of them are in privileged
occupations where they are among a bunch of other white men
and a few other white women. They aren't used to black dominant females."[1]

Putting on a game face every day can be debilitating. It can
leave us feeling alienated from our true selves. Who you are at
work versus who you are at home can become a chasm.

"You have to be this kind of one-dimensional person for
your clients. But just because I'm able to enact these things in
sessions, does not mean that I'm always like this," she said. "I'm
not always on. I'm not always powerful, and you don't want
your clients to see that side of you, because they wouldn't want
to be with you."

Mistress Velvet also told me how she has struggled with
eating disorders for years. It was a way to assert control over
overwhelming feelings.

"There was a lot of pain when I had to admit that to myself, that I'm actually not always powerful and always strong,"
she said. "In my work as a pro-domme, I exude a lot of confi-

dence, but for a time, I wasn't feeling those things about myself. I felt worthless and powerless in my regular life."

Mistress Velvet has a tattoo on her chest that reads "I am enough."

"The tattoo is really personal," she said. "In 2019, I realized I really hadn't been taking care of myself. Now it's written on me that I am worthy, that I am enough, and it's a reminder for me as well as it is for others.

"I think sometimes I feel like Mistress Velvet and my personal life are becoming one, like I am becoming her," she said. "I'm working on it."

Finding peaceful places where we can sit with ourselves and be at peace with our bodies is essential for our survival. Alone time is precious, because it's a time when no one is looking at us. It's a time when we can let down our guard and exist only within our mind's eye. If we can't love our bodies when we're alone, how can we demand that others treat our bodies with the same respect?

"I love swimming," Mistress Velvet told me. "In the past I haven't had a very good relationship with working out, because I can get kind of obsessed with my body. Swimming works for me, it's an act of exercise that makes my knees feel good and gives me purpose, but not in the way that it used to represent during when I had an eating disorder.

"Lately, I've been going to dinner by myself, which can make other people very uncomfortable, because people may think that you don't have any friends to eat with," she said. "There's nothing wrong with eating alone. Having these moments for myself where I really block out everyone, put away my phone, or put my headphones on lets me become absorbed in my world and allows me to reflect."

YOU WILL GIVE YOURSELF
TIME TO HEAL

From the day we're born, our bodies are changing. We're born, we grow up, we hit puberty, we gain weight, we gain muscles. Having kids changes our bodies, as do illnesses and injuries.

Our physical forms don't always cooperate or keep up with our wisdom, which just gets sharper as we get older. We get so much better as we age, and we want the rest of us to keep getting sharper along with our wisdom and confidence.

Goddess Samantha, the dominatrix with a passion for grappling and wrestling, has struggled to come back from the injuries she sustained doing the work she loves.

"I've been called Python Queen because I would just slither around them and constrict slowly and then just choke them near to death," she said. "I just love to wrestle."

All Goddess Samantha's flying feats of superhuman strength have taken a toll on her body. Wrestling grown men all day long can be—pun intended—punishing.

"There's one night I'll never forget. I was in New York City with a bodybuilder friend that I travel with. It had been a long day, wrestling fetish sessions all day long. And when I say all day, I was starting at 10:00 a.m. and I would go till midnight.

"There was one particular day that I had six sessions, which is a *long* day. And I had three of them back-to-back that were wrestling sessions, and not just fluffy wrestling, serious semi-competitive stuff. One wanted hard-core WWE-style wrestling and jujitsu-type wrestling. But they all wanted lift and carries, meaning I would lift them up over my shoulders, carry them around the room, throw them down, wrestle them, and just do it all again.

"And as the day went on, as the night went on, the guys went up in weight. The first guy weighed, like, one sixty-five. The second guy was one seventy-five. And the third one was one eighty-five. My max was two hundred. Normally, one seventy-five was really my limit. But I'm stubborn, and I would do two hundred if I could, just because I wanted to do it.

"So by the end of that night my body was just throbbing and achy. And my legs were Jell-O. I was really feeling it, I was really sore. But I had to do it because I love what I do."

During our phone conversation, she told me about how all the years of wear and tear forced her to have double hip replacements, and the recovery was grueling. The excruciating pain threw her into a deep depression.

"I didn't want to have an operation, but I didn't have a choice because my body was falling apart around me," she said. "I was really angry because the surgery was going to change my life, my career, and the whole nine yards.

"Then I had a setback with the second surgery, I had an impingement in my groin area. That hurt worse than the damn surgery, let me tell you. I had a come-to-Jesus moment one morning. I couldn't sit up. When I would sit up, it literally felt like somebody was taking my vagina inside, grabbing ahold of it, and pulling it out of my body. It hurt so bad.

"Well, I literally cried. I woke up at five in the morning and I just screamed. It was a long day. I prayed, I asked God to help me get through it, to give me a break. I was exhausted from crying from the pain and from being so sad about it all. But the next morning, I woke up, and the pain was gone."

For Goddess Samantha, power comes from moving forward and working to heal from setbacks that take a lot more than just physical therapy. It's about accepting limitations and thriving in her body the way it is today.

"I'm still rebuilding my body. It's not the body I used to have, and I'm not as strong as I used to be. I have to train differently now, which is still hard for me, because my mind-set is still 'lift heavy or go home.' But I know that I just can't.

"But would I do it all over again? Absolutely."

YOU WILL SEEK ROLE MODELS AND MENTORS

Cyndi Lauper was my first role model. I loved her wild red hair with the checkerboard shaved into the side. I loved her crazy plastic jewelry, her makeup, her colorful outfits. MTV played the video for "Girls Just Wanna Have Fun" around the clock, and I just loved those images of Cyndi and her punk rock friends, forcing men to clear a path so they could dance through the streets, and how it ended with a wild party in her bedroom. I didn't understand the poignancy of the lyrics at the time, that she and her mother weren't the fortunate ones, that boys wanted to take a beautiful girl and hide her away from the rest of the world, and how she wanted to be the one to walk in the sun. All I saw was the fun, the joy, the dancing, and that she was an artist and a clear weirdo.

I never shaved my head or danced in the street barefoot in a red strapless dress, but I did become an artist and a weirdo.

In high school, Hillary Clinton and Surgeon General Joycelyn Elders were my role models. Hillary, because she wanted to change health care for Americans, and for being strong and not folding when magazine covers Photoshopped her in dominatrix gear (ah, the irony), lambasted her for daring to have ideas, and for being cool with having a regular, awkward teenage daughter who looked like, well, the rest of us. I thought Joycelyn Elders was awesome for preaching sex education and daring to promote the idea that masturbation was a great alternative to risky sex for teenagers. I didn't know anything about her sexual health work on behalf of women of color, who she felt were not being given the same sex education as white women. I just thought it was terrible that they were both women who were shunted to the side because they said things that men didn't like.

I never ran for office, and I never went to medical school, but I do try to stand firm in my belief that all women and girls deserve agency over their bodies, and that every young person deserves real sex education that speaks to and informs them.

In college, my writing teacher, the author Stephen Mc-Cauley, was a role model. He wrote about emotionally damaged people, but with such humor, love, and empathy that you couldn't help but fall in love with them. He encouraged me to keep writing when I didn't think I was any good. I thought all good writing had to be serious. I didn't feel confident enough to embrace my sense of humor in my writing until we met. He let me hang out in his office for hours, listening to me, encouraging me to keep writing when I didn't think I was any good. He was funny, witty, generous. He was the first adult who really listened to me. The books and authors he recommended to me became my favorites.

He inspired me to become a writer who explores people's shadows, but also their light. And most importantly, he convinced me that the worst thing a person could ever be is boring.

Not all of us are lucky enough to have real-life mentors. We idolize celebrities for their looks and lifestyle because they represent what we want our lives to look like. But choosing a mentor or a guiding light should go further than just declaring a person #goals because they look like they've got it all.

"Pick a person that you admire, the one who has qualities

that inspire you. It's digging deeper than just 'Oh, they're famous and people admire them,'" said Hudsy Hawn. "Instead of saying 'I want to be like Beyoncé,' ask yourself, 'Why am I drawn to Beyoncé's energy?' Sure, she's a kick-ass diva. But why is she a kick-ass diva? What energy is she putting out there, what is she actually doing with her power? Then you can ask yourself how you can become a kick-ass diva too.'"

Every year I add to my list of role models. I edit it, I rethink it. People who "give no fucks" are rad, but I also admire people who give (or gave) very specific fucks about the things they care about. Artists like John Waters, Barbara Loden, Liz Phair, Dawn Powell, David Lynch, Louise Bourgeois, Lynda Barry, Aline Kominsky, Maria Bamford, they all tell me that I'm on the right track, that they can do whatever they're doing and succeed despite struggling or being outsiders, and outliers.

Our role models can disappoint us. They can mislead us. We might realize later in life that they actually gave us lousy advice, or meant well, but really didn't know what they were talking about. Not having a role model can make it hard to navigate personal and professional challenges. Books and blogs may not be enough when we're trying to figure out what we want and how to get there.

"I didn't have any real models when I was exploring the world of kink and BDSM," said Gloria Brame. "I was trying to live up to what I thought I was supposed to be based on what I could find.

"It helped a lot to make friends in the community, because they were regular people who'd been around long enough to know that real life doesn't operate like a fantasy. At the same time, we were all trying to live like Slave O and Sir Stephen out of *The Story of O*. I mean, we were all desperately in search of role models."

You may not have to look as far as you think you do to find

a role model. If there's someone you know whom you admire, tell them. Not only will they probably be super flattered, but, if you ask politely, they may tell you how they got to be who they are—everything it took to get them there.

Expand your ideas about who your role models can be and for what. An aunt who went back to school while raising her kids as a single parent can be a role model for time management and perseverance. A friend who survived cancer can be a role model for strength and keeping a sense of humor during dark times. The woman in your neighborhood who runs her own coffee shop can teach you volumes about courage and entrepreneurship.

"Keep going, keep finding people that impress you, and keep asking yourself why what they say or do resonates with you. It doesn't have to be just kink-related. It can be painting, business, or just how they handle themselves," said Hudsy Hawn. "We can never be [exactly like]our heroes, but we take lessons from them."

Many of the pro-dommes have mentors who've helped them on their path. They credit these women with teaching them not only the skills of the trade but also how to build their businesses, and keep going in a tough business while staying true to themselves.

"I have someone in my life that I'm mentoring right now. She has a lot of self-confidence issues, and one of the things I ask her to do is congratulate herself every day for something she's done, no matter how small," said Lucy Sweetkill. "Like, what does she value about herself that day? What did she do really well or accomplish? And it could be as simple as 'I went to the gym today' or 'I was struggling, but I got out and walked the dog.'"

We all deserve someone to look up to. Just be careful about whom you choose and make sure they're worthy of your admiration.

YOU WILL REACH OUT TO OTHERS

In 2019, pushing back against bad policy, sexism, racism, homophobia, transphobia, cruelty, and apathy seems like a Sisyphean task.

"There's so many things that have to change at the same time to make a real difference," said Lucy Sweetkill. "On this big, macro level, we have to examine how we treat women in general and in our society as a whole. Men can learn to become better allies in supporting women and supporting the oppression of women and their own male toxic behavior."

It sure would be nice not to have to educate the world about how they can make it a better and kinder place.

Making changes on a local level is a good place to start. You can start in your own neighborhood—speak up when you see something awful; step up and help a woman who appears to be in danger, or is being harassed.

"I'm hyperaware and hypervigilant to be an ally to any woman that seems to be having trouble with unwanted male attention," said Dia Domina Dynasty. "I no longer let men talk to me whom I have not welcomed or invited conversation with. My sense of self-worth is no longer based in how I am accepted or welcomed by others, but by how I feel about myself in any situation."

When Mistress Ava Zhang travels to a city, she makes it a point to host events and invite other pro-dommes, especially ones she hasn't met yet. Every new person in the scene inspires her and teaches her.

"I really love to connect with the people in the other cities, and figure out who they are," she said. "It's about making a sisterhood. But it's also essential for my mental health, you know? I also started to really find out who I am and get to know myself, like reintroducing myself to myself in a way. It's so important to find a community of like-minded people so that you don't feel lonesome in this world."

IT'S OKAY TO BE ANGRY

In 2018, Ronan Farrow and Jane Mayer published an article in the *New Yorker* titled "Four Women Accuse New York's Attorney General of Physical Abuse."[2] The article delved into the case of Eric Schneiderman, the most powerful attorney in the state, who was alleged to have "engaged in nonconsensual physical violence," including choking, slapping, intimidating, threatening, and verbally humiliating women he dated. It's a long and well-reported piece, with horrifying details that encompass the entire spectrum of physical abuse masquerading as kink.

In a statement given before he resigned, Schneiderman said, "In the privacy of intimate relationships, I have engaged in role-playing and other consensual sexual activity. I have not assaulted anyone. I have never engaged in nonconsensual sex, which is a line I would not cross."

Tanya Selvaratnam, one of the women who spoke to the *New Yorker* (others reported being too frightened to do so out of fear of retribution), put it differently. "This is a man who has staked his entire career, his personal narrative, on being a champion for women publicly. But he abuses them privately. He needs to be called out."

I had voted for Schneiderman. He seemed like a good guy with a progressive platform that ticked all the boxes: He was pro-choice; he championed the #MeToo movement; he took on big banks over fraudulent foreclosure tactics; he sponsored legislation to protect victims of domestic violence, including the Strangulation Prevention Act,[3] which made the intentional obstruction of breathing or blood circulation a misdemeanor.

In Chelsea G. Summers's 2018 article "The Rub of Rough Sex,"[4] she examines her own relationships to men whose partners "must—as I have, as friends of yours have, as so many women throughout history have—come to the chilling realization that someone they loved and trusted sexually abused them in the name of 'rough sex.'

"I understood the disconnect between thinking you were dating a 'woke' man, a guy who understood in his guts the inequity of being a woman in this patriarchal world, and finding that this man was a rank, abusive hypocrite," she wrote.

We are raised from such a young age to keep quiet, to be nice, to take it with a smile. When we assert ourselves, we're written off with sexist or condescending adjectives like "shrill," "opinionated," "feisty," or "spirited." We're harridans, we're battle-axes, we're bitches, we're cunts, we're not "staying in our lane," we're emotional, we're on the rag, we're psychos, we're "not ladylike," we're nags.

Professional dominatrixes get angry about the way they and other sex workers are portrayed in the media. Conservatives brand them as the dregs of society (while paying for their services on the sly), while liberals treat them as victims that need to be protected, without any thought to what they actually need to be protected *from*, which is harassment, police abuse, and the inability to run their businesses safely and effectively.

Pro-dommes are constantly pushing back at damaging misconceptions about their work. Many of them took to social media to decry the way their industry was portrayed in the Netflix series *Bonding*, which followed a beginner dominatrix's adventures in New York City. The show, they said, played to hackneyed, as well as flat-out false, stereotypes. Instead of showing their community as it really is—the kindness, trust, and healing they do, the regard they have for their clients, and the dangers that come with being a sex worker—the show did a disservice.

Many of the dominatrixes I spoke to for the book were furious that the show didn't take the time to show the negotiation of boundaries and consent, which is intrinsic to their work and to all BDSM play.

"In one episode, she fails to vet a client due to the amount of money he offers her, something that represents extremely risky behavior," Mistress Couple told *Rolling Stone*.[5] "This, above all else, is perhaps the most egregious flaw of *Bonding*—the fact that, for a show about sex work and BDSM, it has no interest in engaging with the reality of what it means to do both safely."

When we ignore and deny our anger, as we're culturally groomed to do, rage can start to manifest in other ways. After a while, resentment can poison every other aspect of our lives.

"Repressed anger can actually make us deeply physically sick. It can become really toxic, and in some cases, really violent," said Dawn Serra. "When we ignore our anger, it can get louder and louder and louder. It feels terrible to keep silent when really, we're just trying to be heard."

A lot of self-help gurus say that the key to happiness is letting go of anger. I say that anger is a part of what keeps us from accepting things we cannot change. It keeps us engaged with the world around us. You can learn to cope with your anger without becoming complacent. You can channel your anger into action.

"I do have this like, medium burning flame of rage," said Mistress Velvet. "So I've just decided to not have shame around it. I've come to terms with it. Like, it's probably going to exist for the rest of my life. And that's okay."

YOU WILL KEEP GROWING

All of the lessons that the pro-dommes shared with me for this book, like all good lessons, came from life experience, deep introspection, and trial and error—not only in their work but also in their personal relationships.

Many of the women I spoke to for this book told me that they have mantras, keep goals, and maintain vision boards. Getting through our days can be a challenge, and confidence can wax and wane. No one is born confident; we all have to give ourselves pep talks during times when we aren't feeling like the person we want to be. Building confidence doesn't happen overnight, for any of us. We don't know who we are when we start out. We don't know where our choices will take us. We can't be sure that it will all work out.

Before Lucy Sweetkill became a dominatrix, she'd already been asking herself hard questions about her sexuality, power, and the kind of world she wanted to live in. She'd already been exploring kink and BDSM on a personal level but wanted to be sure that this was a path she wanted to go down as a professional.

"We as women are not given the tools of confidence when we start out. We're told to kind of diminish ourselves in some capacity, that we're not good enough, and there's lots of comparison to others," said Lucy Sweetkill. "In the beginning I didn't know what being a pro-domme meant outside of myself yet. I didn't know what it meant for my friends, to society, for my culture, for my relationships. I kept what I was doing hidden because I was still working on me.

"When I went public about what I was doing, I had pushback and a lot of judgment from some very close friends. Those were hard lessons. I've had to become strong enough to not let things hurt me in these deep ways."

She told me that she worked hard to transform these challenges into opportunities to find more confidence in her choices and to say no to bad relationships that were no longer serving her evolving needs. She credits this tough time in her life with making her the person she is now, a person who can help others.

"Now I'm in a partnership that's super supportive, that's super loving, because I've learned to love myself through it," she said. "He's learned to love me because I know myself. And I have more fulfilling friendships."

Learning to harness your inner power means having the ability to see yourself as you really are. Only if you face yourself can you really understand what you need to change.

"You have to take a lot of risks, and you have to be honest with yourself, and you have to be able to look at both your good traits and your bad traits," Sweetkill said. "You have to ask yourself, 'What did I do? What did I not do? What could I have done better?' And to keep asking yourself those questions."

We all reckon with our pasts, try to live in the present, and focus on how we can build a future where we're happy, whole, and at peace. We all need a mantra and a place to return to when we forget who we are and what we're capable of.

"If I could talk to twenty-year-old me now, I would say, you will be stronger," said Goddess Samantha. "Because I didn't feel so strong growing up. I'd just tell her to just hang in there and you're going to get stronger mentally and physically and things are going to change. You're going to do amazing things. You're going to be the greatest."

Power starts with believing that you are the guardian of your own destiny. It's an understanding that no one will give you the keys to the kingdom, and if they could, they can just as easily snatch them back. It's being your own best friend and keeper of your dreams. It's coming to the end of your life and being able to tell yourself that despite it all, you did it your way.

EPILOGUE

Picture it: New York City, 2019.

A tall-ish woman quits her job at a tech start-up and takes off on a wild adventure. She dubs it her "year of magical kinking," and gleefully throws herself into the world of dungeons, dominatrix conventions, and deep conversations about power dynamics, sex, and self-love. It's a year filled with laughter, latex, and long nights at the laptop, trying to encapsulate a transformative experience into something that kinky and non-kinky folks alike can relate to. She hands in the final draft and dreams of 2020—a year filled with lectures and readings and openhearted discussions with strangers about desire, confidence, and personal power.

Friends, as you've probably guessed, that is not the way that 2020 unfolded.

Instead, the national conversation would be all about power—but on a life-and-death scale. In March and April, COVID-19 ravaged my beloved New York City. In May, angry Americans took to the streets to protest Breonna Taylor's and George Floyd's deaths. In 2020, was there a single person who didn't question the whole notion of power, and who holds the strings when it comes to our health, personal safety, and financial well-being, not to mention the future of our democracy?

I had to ask myself: In a time of national upheaval, when our very lives are at stake, did a book on kinky thinking matter?

I'm writing this updated epilogue from my couch, cat in lap, six months into a pandemic that made mincemeat out of my plans (and, most likely, yours as well). And all I can tell you is that the lessons from this book are actually exactly what sustained me this year. They helped me come to terms with the fact that this year would not be the celebratory "year of magical kinking" that would take me on a cross-country adventure. They helped me and my husband navigate tough conversations about finances and professional anxiety. They helped me get up the courage to go back to work, something I had not planned to do in 2020. They made me the person I am today—a better, wiser, and more controlled version of myself than I was in 2018, when I was too scared to pitch a book, any book, let alone one that would take me to such scary, thrilling, and heart-bending places.

The women I spoke to for this book taught me a lot of valuable lessons. Here are a few of my favorites.

AM I BEING SERVED?

I'm not talking about customer service. I'm talking about relationships, friendships, jobs, and situations that used to work for me but now do not. In the past, I felt shame for giving up on something after having invested so much of my heart. I blamed myself for going down the wrong path and questioned my judgment as a result.

Writing about the Kardashians wasn't serving me spiritually. The grueling breaking-news cycle and reporting the horrors of the day weren't serving my emotional health. Working overnight shifts, eating out of snack machines, and sitting at a desk all day weren't serving my physical health. I hadn't gotten a raise in years, so my work certainly wasn't serving me financially. Maybe my employers didn't owe me anything but a paycheck, but I owed myself so much more.

But I realized, I wasn't wrong for having felt hopeful and passionate about those things at the time. I'd been way too hard on myself. The world changed quickly and unexpectedly; journalism, the career I had studied for, changed radically. The best-laid career plans don't always work out—something we all face at some point. I had this idea in my head that other people were doing it better than me. But, in truth, I'd had enough of putting my heart into a career that wasn't working for me.

It's only human to feel disappointment. But walking away to pursue something better and more meaningful isn't quitting. It's wising up.

NO ONE WILL DIE IF I SAY "NO"

There have been so many times in my life where I've thought, *There's no way in hell I'm going to be able to do that,* while hearing myself say, "Sure, sounds great!" Why was I so afraid to say "no" to asinine ideas—midnight karaoke on a work night, a birthday dinner at a ludicrously overpriced restaurant where I didn't know anyone, or networking drinks with a person I didn't even want to see? I once agreed to train for a 5K just to get someone off my back. Friends, I do not, and will never, enjoy running.

I was afraid of confrontation. I wanted people to think I

was nice, reliable, and easygoing. So what if I was miserable? I was liked! It was easier to be mad at myself than to have someone else be mad at me.

Since putting the strategies in this book into practice, I've been starting small, but seeing real results. It's mostly minor stuff for now, but meaningful. In 2020, I said "no" to outdoor birthday parties during COVID, getting on a plane for a wedding (that sucked), and listening to people complain about wearing masks. Recommended!

HAVE TO SAY IT, NOT PRAY IT

Sulking is unproductive, friends. We can't expect the ones we love to read our minds. When it comes to getting what I want, I need to vocalize exactly what I need, and why. There have been so many times when I've been furious because my husband should have "just known" that I was upset or overwhelmed.

If I can't vocalize that I'm annoyed or upset, how can I expect the other person to know how to respond?

There's no one-size-fits-all guide to making a long-term committed relationship work. It's easy to talk about honest communication, but putting it into practice is *hard*. I took all the lessons in this book to heart and, more important, put them to the test. None of it was easy. I can say now that my husband and I no longer fear that the other person will leave if we dare ask for things that may not fly in other marriages. As the (true) cliché goes, every couple is different. No one else can, or should, tell you how to make your relationship work. My best advice is that you both have to start saying "I want." And then listen—and keep listening.

PUTTING MYSELF FIRST ISN'T THE SAME THING AS BEING SELFISH

I'd always had an eye-rolling aversion to the phrase "self-care." It seemed so narcissistic and indulgent. Who was I to rub essential oils on my temples and meditate when there was so much suffering in the world? I equated "self-care" with selfishness. It was for people who referred to their lives as "journeys" and thought of their yoga practice as being helpful to humanity.

In 2020, I was even angry at people posting about "self-care" on social media. Did they think that their sourdough starters and meditation were going to cure COVID? But then, after a lot of introspection, I realized that I was sort of jealous. I was having trouble coping; how dare they have a moment of pleasure? I decided then and there that I was going to stop being so judgy and start taking more bubble baths. I knew that they wouldn't keep the specter of COVID and all the nerve-racking uncertainty that came with it at bay, not really, but it was okay to enjoy a moment of peace, especially if it gave me the energy to fight another day.

Self-care isn't just pedicures, crystal facials, and pashmina wraps. It can mean admitting when you need a major time-out. A bath bomb can't cure career burnout, or fix all the reasons why I struggle to get to sleep at night. Real self-care isn't a product or service you can buy with a Groupon. It's work, and it isn't always pretty. It's a commitment to understanding yourself and working to change things for the better.

People will respect me more if I . . .

Accept compliments

Acknowledge my accomplishments

Don't apologize when I haven't done anything wrong

Put guardrails around my time

Choose not to engage with people I deem to be unworthy of my energy

Say what I mean and not what I think others want to hear

Answer emails and texts when I actually have a response instead of always being available

Don't reveal my faults to make others feel better about theirs

Acknowledge my mistakes gracefully

Don't try to solve other people's problems

Am gracious in victory

I DESERVE TO GO AFTER WHAT I WANT

Some people have power handed to them as part of their inheritance. Those people don't need to be taught how to act and speak more powerfully, because they've been raised to believe that the world should bow down to them. That doesn't mean those people are happy or fulfilled. It doesn't mean that they are loved for themselves or respected for who they are as humans.

The things I want aren't so insane. I don't want fancy cars or a private jet. I don't need to stay at the Four Seasons when I travel and own homes in glamorous cities all over the world. I don't want to be famous or the life of every party (just some parties). I just want to be comfortable. I want time to myself. I want to laugh more than cry. I want great sex. I want adventure. I want to grow old with my husband and friends. I want to be creative for a living as often as I can.

None of this requires a fairy godmother or a billion dollars. It just requires hard work, a lot of self-examination, and a little luck. All I need is a vision and the belief that, heck, I deserve it. After all, no one will fight for me the way I will.

When I first started writing this book, I wanted professional dominatrixes to teach me how to demand respect from others. To my surprise, what I actually learned was how to start valuing myself and respecting my gifts and talents. I learned how to come to the table with all I have to offer instead of worrying about all the things I lack. Now when someone tells me that they admire me for summoning up my courage, quitting my job, and taking such a crazy professional risk, I gladly accept the praise. I mean, I did all those things! And besides, who am I to argue with their good taste?

ACKNOWLEDGMENTS

In addition to those who spoke to me for this book, there are so many people who helped and offered encouragement, love, support, pep talks, and insights via phone, text, and in person when I needed it most.

In no particular order: Simone Justice, the organizers and attendees of DomCon, Sarah Robbins, Jeremy Stulberg, Jason Gordon, Karen Duffy, Matt Hamilton, Graeme Wood, Margaux Neiderbach, Jeremy Quittner, Lola a.k.a. MD, Mary Kelly, Stephen McCauley, Claudia Krugovoy, Anjali Khosla, Ethan Sacks, Joanna Molloy, Dennis Cohen, Jonathan Lang, Autumn Whitefield-Madrano, Catey Hill, Seth Rosenblatt, all the Goldwerts, and the rest of my extended family.

Special thanks to Theresa DiMasi, Anja Schmidt, and Emily Carleton at Tiller Press, Iris Blasi and the Carol Mann Agency, and to the Paragraph writers' space in NYC for giving me a quiet place to work. And finally to Tim Heffernan, for everything.

FURTHER READING

Below, you'll find a list of works that I've cited in this book, plus a few more that have inspired me along the way.

50 Shades of Kink: An Introduction to BDSM by Tristan Taormino

Anything for You: Erotica for Kinky Couples by Rachel Kramer Bussell (all the anthologies she's edited are great)

The Body Is Not an Apology: The Power of Radical Self-Love by Sonya Renee Taylor

The Corporate Dominatrix: Six Roles to Play to Get Your Way at Work by Lisa Robyn

Eloquent Rage: A Black Feminist Discovers Her Superpower by Brittney Cooper

The Ethical Slut: A Practical Guide to Polyamory, Open Relationships, and Other Freedoms in Sex and Love by Janet W. Hardy and Dossie Easton

Face Value: The Hidden Ways Beauty Shapes Women's Lives by Autumn Whitefield-Madrano

Invisible Women: Data Bias in a World Designed for Men by Caroline Criado Perez

A Lover's Pinch: A Cultural History of Sadomasochism by Peter Tupper

Mating in Captivity: Unlocking Erotic Intelligence by Esther Perel

The Mistress Manual: The Good Girl's Guide to Female Dominance by Mistress Lorelei Powers

The New Bottoming Book by Dossie Easton and Janet W. Hardy

The New Topping Book by Dossie Easton and Janet W. Hardy

The Nice Girl's Guide to Talking Dirty: Ignite Your Sex Life With Naughty Whispers, Hot Fantasies and Screams of Passion by Ruth Neustifter, PhD

The Sexually Dominant Woman by Lady Green

Sister Outsider: Essays and Speeches by Audre Lorde

Tell Me What You Want: The Science of Sexual Desire and How It Can Help You Improve Your Sex Life by Justin J. Lehmiller

Thinking Kink: The Collision of BDSM, Feminism and Popular Culture by Catherine Scott

The Ultimate Guide to Bondage: Creating Intimacy Through the Art of Restraint by Mistress Couple

The Ultimate Guide to Kink: BDSM, Role Play and the Erotic Edge by Tristan Taormino

Vox by Nicholson Baker

Waking the Witch: Reflections on Women, Magic, and Power by Pam Grossman

When Someone You Love Is Kinky by Dossie Easton and Catherine A. Liszt

Whip Smart: The True Story of a Secret Life by Melissa Febos

Wild Side Sex: The Book of Kink by Midori

Women & Power: A Manifesto by Mary Beard

Women on Top by Nancy Friday

Advocacy

Decriminalize Sex Work; Decriminalizesex.work
Sex Workers Project; Sexworkersproject.org
Sex Workers Outreach Project USA; swopusa.org
Global Network of Sex Work Projects; nswp.org

NOTES

WHAT IS A DOMINATRIX?

1   Michael Aaron, PhD, "BDSM as Harm Reduction," *Psychology Today*, October 13, 2016, accessed August 5, 2019, https://www.psychologytoday.com/us/blog/standard-devia
tions/201610/bdsm-harm-reduction.

2   Hannah M. E. Rogak and Jennifer Jo Connor, "Practice of Consensual BDSM and Relationship Satisfaction," *Sexual and Relationship Therapy* 33, no 4 (2018), accessed August 5, 2019, https://www.tandfonline.com/doi/abs/10.1080/14681994.20
17.1419560.

THE POWER OF THE WORD

LESSON #1: KINKY WORDS ARE LIFE WORDS

1   Author interview with Tina Horn.

2   Tristan Taormino, ed., *The Ultimate Guide to Kink: BDSM, Role Play and the Erotic Edge* (Berkeley, CA: Cleis Press, 2012).

3   Author interview with Tina Horn.

4   Author interview with Mistress Couple.

5   Nidhi Prakash, "Joe Biden Made Multiple Jokes About Consent in His First Speech Since Allegations of Inappropriate

Contact," BuzzFeed News, April 5, 2019, accessed August 5, 2019, https://www.buzzfeednews.com/article/nidhiprakash/joe-biden-2020-physical-contact-joke.

6   Thomas Beaumont and Nicholas Riccardi, "Biden Jokes about Accusations, Targets Union Voters," Associated Press, April 5, 2019, https://www.apnews.com/f9bb1b8c385044ffb74b2c725c3dd83b.

7   Mistress Couple, *The Ultimate Guide to Bondage: Creating Intimacy Through the Art of Restraint* (New York: Cleis Press, 2018).

LESSON #2: YOU MUST SPEAK WITH AUTHORITY

1   Kieran Snyder, "Women Should Watch Out for This One Word in Their Reviews," *Fortune*, December 3, 2014, accessed August 5, 2019, http://fortune.com/2014/08/26/performance-review-gender-bias/.

2   Caroline Criado Perez, *Invisible Women: Data Bias in a World Designed for Men* (New York: Abrams Press, 2019).

3   Ibid.

4   Ibid.

5   Author interview with Hudsy Hawn.

6   Lisa Robyn, *The Corporate Dominatrix: Six Roles to Play to Get Your Way at Work* (New York: Simon & Schuster, 2007).

LESSON #3: YOU WILL LEARN TO COMMUNICATE YOUR DESIRE

1   Author interview with Brianna Rader.

2   Josh Feldman, "Awkward: Bill O'Reilly Grills Students Behind University of Tennessee's 'Sex Week,'" *Mediaite*, March 22, 2013, https://www.mediaite.com/tv/awkward-bill-oreilly-grills-students-behind-university-of-tennessees-sex-week/.

3   Ruth Neustifter, *The Nice Girl's Guide to Talking Dirty: Ignite Your Sex Life with Naughty Whispers, Hot Fantasies, and Screams of Passion* (Berkeley, CA: Amorata Press, 2011).

4   Author interview with Gloria Brame.

THE POWER OF THE MIND
LESSON #4: YOU MAY HAVE TWO NAMES

1   Author interview with Goddess Samantha.

LESSON #5: YOUR INTUITION IS A SUPERPOWER

1   Daniel G. Amen, Manuel Trujillo, David Keator, et al., "Gender-Based Cerebral Perfusion Differences in 46,034 Functional Neuroimaging Scans," *Journal of Alzheimer's Disease* 60, no. 2 (2017): 605–14.

2   Renee Morad, "Women's Intuition: It's a Real Thing, Ask a Neuroscientist," Ozy.com, September 17, 2017.

3   Katherine J. Wu, "Between the (Gender) Lines: The Science of Transgender Identity," SITN, October 25, 2016, http://sitn.hms .harvard.edu/flash/2016/gender-lines-science-transgender-identity/.

4   Lise Eliot, "Neurosexism: The Myth That Men and Women Have Different Brains," *Nature* 566 (2019): 453–54.

5   Pam Grossman, *Waking the Witch: Reflections on Women, Magic, and Power* (New York: Gallery Books, 2019).

6   Author interview with Madame Rose.

7   https://www.congress.gov/bill/115th-congress/house-bill /1865/text.

8   https://www.congress.gov/bill/115th-congress/senate-bill /1693.

9   Lura Chamberlain, "FOSTA: A Hostile Law with a Human Consequence," *Fordham Law Review* 87 (5) (2019), https://ir.lawnet .fordham.edu/cgi/viewcontent.cgi?article=5598&context=flr.

10 Aaron Mackey and Elliot Harmon, "Congress Censors the Internet, But EFF Continues to Fight FOSTA: 2018 in Review," EFF, December 29, 2018, https://www.eff.org/deeplinks/2018/12/con gress-censors-internet-eff-continues-fight-fosta-2018-review.

THE POWER OF THE BODY
LESSON #7: YOUR BODY DESERVES WORSHIP

1   Sonya Renee Taylor, *The Body Is Not an Apology: The Power of Radical Self Love* (Oakland, CA: Berret-Koehler Publications, 2018).

2 Author interview with Dawn Serra.

3 "Identity Documents," Lambda Legal, n.d., accessed August 5, 2019, https://www.lambdalegal.org/know-your-rights/article /trans-identity-documents.

4 Elise Viebeck, "A Brief Recap of 'Tampongate,' the Week's Strangest Controversy on Capitol Hill," *Washington Post*, June 29, 2018, accessed August 5, 2019, https://www .washingtonpost.com/news/powerpost/wp/2018/06/29/a -brief-recap-of-tampongate-the-weeks-strangest-controversy -on-capitol-hill/?noredirect=on&utm_term=.abe25782ed65.

5 Ibid.

6 Katrin Bennhold, "Another Side of #MeToo: Male Managers Fearful of Mentoring Women," *New York Times*, January 27, 2019, accessed August 5, 2019, https://www.nytimes .com/2019/01/27/world/europe/metoo-backlash-gender -equality-davos-men.html.

7 Gillian Tan and Katia Porzecanski, "Wall Street Rule for the #MeToo Era: Avoid Women at All Cost," Bloomberg.com, December 3, 2018, accessed August 5, 2019, https://www .bloomberg.com/news/articles/2018-12-03/a-wall-street-rule -for-the-metoo-era-avoid-women-at-all-cost.

8 Ashley Parker, "Karen Pence Is the Vice President's 'Prayer Warrior,' Gut Check and Shield," *Washington Post*, March 28, 2017, accessed August 5, 2019, https://www.washingtonpost .com/politics/karen-pence-is-the-vice-presidents-prayer-war rior-gut-check-and-shield/2017/03/28/3d7a26ce-0a01-11e7 -8884-96e6a6713f4b_story.html?utm_term=.ea0c38621563.

9 Criado Perez, *Invisible Women*.

10 Autumn Whitefield-Madrano, *Face Value: The Hidden Ways Beauty Shapes Women's Lives* (New York: Simon & Schuster, 2016).

11 Ami R. Zota and Bhavna Shamasunder, "The Environmental Injustice of Beauty: Framing Chemical Exposures from Beauty Products as a Health Disparities Concern," *American Journal of Obstetrics and Gynecology* 217, no. 4 (October 2017): 418. e1–418.e6.

12 Susan Johnston Taylor, "The Pink Tax: Why Women's Products Often Cost More," *U.S. News & World Report*, February 17, 2016, accessed August 5, 2019, https://money.usnews.com

/money/personal-finance/articles/2016-02-17/the-pink-tax
-why-womens-products-often-cost-more.

13 U.S. Department of Health and Human Services, "Fact Sheet: Final Rules on Religious and Moral Exemptions and Accommodation for Coverage of Certain Preventive Services Under the Affordable Care Act," HHS.gov, November 7, 2018, accessed August 5, 2019, https://www.hhs.gov/about/news/2018/11/07/fact-sheet-final-rules-on-religious-and-moral-exemptions-and-accommodation-for-coverage-of-certain-preventive-services-under-affordable-care-act.html.

14 "CBS News Goes Undercover to Reveal Gender Price Discrimination," CBS News, January 25, 2016, accessed August 5, 2019, https://www.cbsnews.com/news/price-discrimination-gender-gap-cbs-news-undercover-dry-cleaners/.

15 New York City Department of Consumer Affairs, "From Cradle to Cane: The Cost of Being a Female Consumer," December 15, 2015, accessed August 5, 2019, https://www1.nyc.gov/site/dca/partners/gender-pricing-study.page.

16 Ibid.

LESSON #8: YOUR CLOTHING GIVES YOU POWER

1 Author interview with The Baroness.

2 Bianca Nieves, "This Trend Has Been Around Since 2500 BCE," *Refinery29*, August 24, 2017, accessed August 5, 2019, https://www.refinery29.com/en-us/2017/08/169562/hoop-earrings-trend-history.

LESSON #9: YOU HOLD YOUR OWN SEXUAL POWER

1 Anna Fitzpatrick, "People Keep Asking Google How to Give a Woman an Orgasm," *Vice*, October 16, 2017, accessed August 5, 2019, https://www.vice.com/en_us/article/mb7mqn/people-keep-asking-google-how-to-give-a-woman-an-orgasm.

2 Sara B. Chadwick and Sari M. van Anders, "Do Women's Orgasms Function as a Masculinity Achievement for Men?," *The Journal of Sex Research* 54, no. 9 (2017): 1141–51, accessed

August 5, 2019, https://www.tandfonline.com/doi/full/10.1080/00224499.2017.1283484.

3 Janet W. Hardy and Dossie Easton, *The Ethical Slut: A Practical Guide to Polyamory, Open Relationships, and Other Freedoms in Sex and Love*, 3rd ed. (Berkeley, CA: Ten Speed Press, 2017).

THE POWER OF DESIRE
LESSON #10: YOU CAN DOMINATE IN THE BEDROOM

1 Midori, "Fortfemme: The Art and Desire of Feminine Dominance," in *The Ultimate Guide to Kink: BDSM, Role Play and the Erotic Edge*, ed. Tristan Taormino (Berkeley, CA: Cleis Press, 2012).

2 Mona Chalabi, "How Many Women Earn More Than Their Husbands?," FiveThirtyEight, February 5, 2015, accessed August 5, 2019, https://fivethirtyeight.com/features/how-many-women-earn-more-than-their-husbands/.

3 Mistress Couple, *The Ultimate Guide to Bondage: Creating Intimacy Through the Art of Restraint* (New York: Cleis Press, 2018).

THE POWER OF THE SPIRIT
LESSON #12: YOU SHALL LIVE BY A CODE

1 Quotes taken from author interview with Mistress Ava Zhang.

LESSON #13: YOU ARE ALWAYS
A WORK IN PROGRESS

1 Author interview with Mistress Velvet.

2 Jane Mayer and Ronan Farrow, "Four Women Accuse New York's Attorney General of Physical Abuse," *The New Yorker*, May 8, 2018, accessed August 5, 2019, https://www.newyorker.com/news/news-desk/four-women-accuse-new-yorks-attorney-general-of-physical-abuse.

3 "Domestic Violence Victims, Law Enforcement Officials and Advocates Join Senator Schneiderman to Support Strangulation Prevention Act," New York State Senate, October 5, 2015,

accessed August 5, 2019, https://www.nysenate.gov/newsroom /press-releases/eric-t-schneiderman/domestic-violence-victims -law-enforcement-officials-and.

4   Chelsea G. Summers, "The Rub of Rough Sex," Longreads, July 24, 2018, accessed August 5, 2019, https://longreads .com/2018/07/25/the-rub-of-rough-sex/.

5   EJ Dickson, "Sex Workers Aren't Happy with the New Net-flix Show About Dominatrixes," *Rolling Stone*, April 29, 2019, https://www.rollingstone.com/culture/culture-features/bond ing-dominatrix-show-netflix-sex-workers-reaction-828552/.

INDEX

Note: Page references in italics indicate illustrations.